From My Kitchen to Yours

Eat Well-

Chef
Jamie

JAMIE GWEN

GOOD FOOD FOR

GOOD TIMES

SIMPLE RECIPES FOR SENSATIONAL CELEBRATIONS

WITH LANA SILLS

Visit www.chefjamie.com for more mouthwatering recipes,
Chef's tips and delicious ideas to make your celebrations come alive with flavor.

Published in association with:
Powerline Publishing Group
Delray Beach, Florida

Food Photography provided by:
Bob Hodson Photography
www.studiohodson.com

Printed in the USA

For My Mommy, whose exceptional talent, support and encouragement
make our collaborations a success to celebrate.
With endless love and gratitude.
~ Jamie ~

For My Jamie, who I love even more than food and cooking.
I'm so happy to share the kitchen with your
marvelous talent and smiling face.
You bring me bliss daily.
~ Lana ~

INTRODUCTION

"Good Food for Good Times" is the second cookbook of irresistible recipes in our Celebration Series.   The word "celebrate" is defined as "A joyful occasion for special festivities to mark some happy event; any joyous diversion...(with fabulous food!)." We hope you will find yourself opening this book for all of the special occasions in your life! These new celebrations include a combination of parties for merriment, togetherness, triumph, success and pure summer fun!

Our passion for cooking has always been tied to the enjoyment others receive from it. There is nowhere else we would rather be, than in the kitchen creating memories of wonderful dishes with family and friends.

We end the book the way we like to end a meal ---- With a Toast to time spent together, joyfully eating and drinking, and to the times yet to be spent celebrating. We hope you enjoy these delicious recipes as much as we do!

Jamie Gwen & Lana Sills

TABLE OF CONTENTS

A Birthday Bash Brunch

CLASSIC GAZPACHO

PUMPKIN GINGER PANCAKES

THE VERY BEST DUTCH BABY

BRIE and HERB STRATA

OLIVE OIL CAKE with 7-MINUTE CURD

7-MINUTE LEMON, ORANGE or PASSIONFRUIT CURD

CLASSIC GAZPACHO Serves 6 to 8

To give this zesty, refreshing chilled soup extra heat, substitute a minced jalapeno for the Tabasco. This very simple recipe is easy to make and allows for lots of variations… Stir in or top the soup with shrimp or crab claws, homemade croutons or chopped, toasted almonds. Gazpacho is ideal for entertaining since it improves when refrigerated overnight.

4 cups tomato juice

1 (14 ounce) can diced tomatoes in puree

1/2 red onion, diced

2 cucumbers, peeled & diced

1 yellow bell pepper, diced

1 red bell pepper, diced

2 garlic cloves, minced

1 tablespoon balsamic vinegar

2 to 3 tablespoons Sherry wine vinegar

1/2 teaspoon Worcestershire sauce

1/2 teaspoon Tabasco

1 teaspoon ground cumin

1/4 cup extra-virgin olive oil

Salt & freshly ground pepper

Garnish: diced avocado, chopped fresh cilantro, lime wedges

Combine all of the ingredients in a large mixing bowl or pitcher. Chill thoroughly before serving.

Serve in chilled cups or bowls garnished with diced avocado, chopped cilantro and a lime wedge.

CHEF'S TIP:
For a quick and easy shortcut (with a pureed consistency),use a food processor to chop and combine all of the ingredients.

PUMPKIN GINGER PANCAKES Makes about 2 dozen Pancakes

This recipe delivers light, fluffy and very flavorful pancakes. They are delicious any season of the year but taste especially good on a cold winter morning during the holidays.

2 cups all-purpose flour	Pinch of salt
1/4 cup firmly packed brown sugar	1 large egg
2 teaspoons baking powder	1/2 cup plain yogurt
1 teaspoon baking soda	3/4 cup whole milk
1 teaspoon ground ginger	3/4 cup canned pumpkin puree
1/2 teaspoon ground cinnamon	2 tablespoons unsalted butter, melted
1/4 teaspoon ground nutmeg	Additional melted butter, for greasing the pan
	Sweet Ginger Butter (recipe follows)
	Warm Maple Syrup

In a mixing bowl, sift together the flour, salt, sugar, baking powder, baking soda, ginger, cinnamon and nutmeg. In a separate bowl, combine the egg, yogurt, milk, pumpkin puree and melted butter. Add the flour mixture to the wet mixture and stir just until blended. Do not over mix!

Heat a pancake griddle or frying pan over medium heat. To test the temperature, a drop of water flicked on the pan should jump about. Brush the pan with a thin layer of melted butter. Pour the batter by scant 1/4 cupfuls and cook the pancakes on the first side until bubbles appear on the surface of the pancakes.

Flip the pancakes with a spatula and cook until golden brown and cooked through, 1 to 2 minutes more. Transfer the pancakes to a large plate and loosely cover with foil to keep warm, then repeat with remaining pancake batter, brushing the skillet with butter before cooking each batch.

Serve the pancakes with Sweet Ginger Butter and warm maple syrup.

SWEET GINGER BUTTER

1/4 cup candied ginger, finely chopped
1 stick (4 ounces) unsalted butter, softened

Combine the ginger and butter together and blend well.

THE VERY BEST DUTCH BABY Serves 8

The perfect breakfast or brunch treat! Bring this spectacular dish to the table as soon as it comes out of the oven for lots of oohs and aahs. A Dutch Baby or German Pancake is a cross between a soufflé and an omelet.

6 eggs, room temperature

1 cup milk, room temperature

1 cup all-purpose flour

3 tablespoons butter

1/2 teaspoon vanilla

1/2 teaspoon ground cinnamon

Pinch of salt

Powdered Sugar, Caramelized Apples, Jam, Whipped Cream

Preheat the oven to 450°F. Place a 10-inch cast iron skillet or ovenproof frying pan in the oven to preheat. While the pan is heating, prepare your batter.

In a large bowl, beat the eggs until light and frothy. Add the milk, flour, vanilla, cinnamon and salt. Beat well to combine. The batter will be thin, but smooth and creamy.

Carefully remove the hot skillet from the oven and add the butter to coat the skillet. Pour the prepared batter into the hot skillet, all at once, and immediately return the skillet to the oven. Bake for 15 to 20 minutes or until puffed and golden brown.

Serve the Dutch Baby immediately dusted with powdered sugar or topped with caramelized apples, jam, whipped cream...etc.!

BRIE and HERB STRATA Serves 8 to 10

This do-ahead dish is simply a savory bread pudding. For extra richness, try using croissants in place of French bread, Cambozola cheese (a blue-veined brie) in place of the triple cream brie and half & half in place of the milk.

> 2 (1 pound) loaves French bread, crusts trimmed & cut into
>   3/4-inch-thick slices
> 4 cups whole milk
> 8 large eggs
> 1 pound Brie cheese, chilled, rind removed
>   and cut into 1/2-inch pieces
> 1/2 cup freshly chopped herbs (parsley, chives, tarragon)
> 1/2 cup grated Parmesan cheese
> 4 tablespoons unsalted butter
> Salt & freshly ground pepper

Butter one large or two medium-sized casserole dishes (no more than 3-inches tall). Place the bread in a large mixing bowl. Pour the milk over the bread and let it soak until soft, about 10 minutes. Squeeze the bread slices over the same bowl, extracting as much milk as possible. Transfer the bread to another mixing bowl. Add the eggs to the milk and whisk to combine to make the custard mixture. Season with salt and pepper.

Place half of the bread mixture in the prepared casserole dish and pour 1/3 of the custard mixture over the top. Allow the custard to seep into the open spaces between the bread. Top with the remaining bread mixture and another 1/3 of the milk mixture (you might not need all of the custard mixture; judge accordingly). Sprinkle the Parmesan cheese over the top and dot with the butter.

BRIE and HERB STRATA continued

Preheat the oven to 350°F. Bake the strata uncovered, until puffed and golden brown, about 1 hour and 15 minutes for a large casserole or 45 minutes for small casseroles. Let the strata cool for 10 minutes before serving. Cut into wedges and serve.

CHEF'S TIP:

Add the brie cheese pieces and chopped herbs to the soaked bread and toss to combine.
(The Strata can be made 1 day ahead. Cover and chill, then bring to room temperature before baking.)

OLIVE OIL CAKE with 7-MINUTE CURD Serves 8

Using extra virgin olive oil in this cake results in a fruity and rich flavor. The 7-Minute Curd is so delicious, so luscious and so versatile you can spread it on anything! The cool, satiny texture of the curd is wonderful on scones hot from the oven or as a delicious filling for cakes, cookies and tarts.

3 large eggs, beaten

2 cups granulated sugar

1/2 cup extra virgin olive oil

1 1/4 cups milk

1/4 cup orange liqueur

1/4 cup fresh orange juice

3 teaspoons lemon zest

2 cups all-purpose flour

1/2 teaspoon baking soda

1/2 teaspoon baking powder

1 teaspoon kosher salt

4 ounces blanched almonds, finely chopped

Garnish: Powdered sugar

Preheat the oven to 350°F. Butter a 10-inch cake pan.

In a large bowl, whisk together the eggs, sugar, olive oil, milk, liqueur, orange juice and lemon zest. Sift together the flour, baking soda, baking powder and salt. Mix the dry mixture into the wet mixture. Whisk until well blended. Fold in the almonds.

Pour the mixture into the buttered cake pan. Bake for 1 hour. Place on a rack to cool completely. Run a knife around the edges to remove the cake and place it on a serving platter. Sprinkle with powdered sugar and serve with the Curd.

7-MINUTE LEMON, ORANGE
or PASSIONFRUIT CURD Makes 1 1/2 cups of Curd

Curd is a deliciously tart, thick but spreadable dessert sauce. This foolproof recipe produces creamy, smooth curd that will last a few weeks in the refrigerator. The recipe can easily be doubled.

1/2 cup freshly squeezed lemon or orange juice
   or strained Passionfruit juice
1 stick (4 ounces) unsalted butter
1/2 cup granulated sugar
1 whole egg
3 egg yolks
Pinch of Salt

Place the lemon, orange or passionfruit juice and the butter in a saucepan over low heat and stir until the butter is melted. Whisk together the sugar, whole egg and yolks and add it to the butter mixture. Stir constantly over low heat for 7 minutes or until the mixture thickens and coats the back of a spoon. Season with a pinch of salt. Ladle the curd into canning jars or store the curd in an airtight container in the refrigerator until ready to use.

"THE PLAYOFFS" PARTY

CHICKEN WINGS with MANGO MOJITO BBQ SAUCE

~~~

SAUSAGES with APPLE KRAUT

~~~

CHIPOTLE PORK CHILI

~~~

SKILLET CORNBREAD with CHIPOTLE BUTTER

~~~

GROWN-UP RICE KRISPY TREATS

CHICKEN WINGS with
MANGO MOJITO BBQ SAUCE Serves 6 to 8

Use this delicious sauce as a marinade and a finishing sauce for grilled meat, chicken or shrimp. You can substitute peaches for the mangoes and add peach liqueur for more flavor.

1/4 cup firmly packed brown sugar

Juice of 6 limes

3 tablespoons freshly grated ginger

2 green onions, chopped

1/4 cup fresh chopped cilantro or mint

4 medium mangoes, peeled and flesh pureed

Salt & freshly ground pepper

1/4 cup Rum

4 pounds chicken wings, wing tips cut off and discarded

Combine all of the ingredients, except the rum, in a saucepot and bring to a simmer over low heat. Cook for 5 minutes to melt the sugar. Remove from the heat, add the rum and let cool.

Preheat the oven to 450°F. Toss the wings with salt and pepper. Line a large casserole dish with aluminum foil and spread the wings in a single layer in the pan. Roast the wings for 20 to 25 minutes, or until cooked through.

Remove the wings from the oven and preheat the broiler to high. Pour half of the prepared sauce into the pan and toss the wings to coat.

Broil the wings for 3 minutes or until golden brown, then turn the wings over and broil 2 minutes more. Brush the wings with additional sauce again before serving and serve remaining sauce alongside for dipping. Be sure to bring the marinade to a full rolling boil for one minute before serving it as a dipping sauce.

SAUSAGES with APPLE KRAUT <small>Serves 4</small>

We recommend that you accompany this dish with coarse grain mustard and offer the beer that you cooked with as the drink of choice. Using a dark beer results in a deep, caramelized flavor. You can add crisp bacon, sautéed onions or juniper berries for additional flavor.

6 assorted fully cooked Polish or German sausages

1 16 ounce bag of sauerkraut, drained

1 green apple, cored and diced

1 tablespoon molasses

1 tablespoon granulated sugar

1 teaspoon caraway seeds

1/2 cup German beer or your beer of choice

4 crusty rolls, split

Preheat the oven to 350°F. Slice the sausages in half lengthwise. Combine the remaining ingredients and toss to combine. Place the sauerkraut mixture in the bottom of a casserole dish and top with the sausages.

Cover the pan with aluminum foil and bake for 45 minutes.
Spoon the sausages and the kraut into toasted rolls and serve.

CHIPOTLE PORK CHILI Serves 6

Chipotle chilies are dried and smoked jalapeños that pack a punch. We love to use the chipotle-infused adobo sauce they come packed in for barbeque sauces, dressings, chili and stews in moderation. You can substitute ground chicken or ground turkey for the pork.

3 tablespoons olive oil

1 yellow onion, diced

2 pounds boneless pork chops, cut into bite-size cubes

1 garlic clove, minced

1 teaspoon dried oregano

2 teaspoons adobo sauce from a can of Chipotles in Adobo, or to taste

1 (15 1/2-ounce) can pinto beans

1 (15 1/2-ounce) can kidney beans

1 (14 1/2-ounce) can beef broth

1 (14 1/2-ounce) can diced tomatoes in juice

1 (4 ounce) can chopped green chilies

1 (8 ounce) can tomato sauce

Salt & freshly ground pepper

Garnish: shredded Pepper Jack Cheese & sour cream

In a large pot, heat the oil over medium heat. Season the pork cubes with salt and pepper and add them to the pot. Sauté, stirring often, until golden brown on all sides. Remove the pork from the pot and add the onion. Season with salt and pepper and sauté until translucent, about 10 minutes. Add the pork back to the pot along with the garlic, oregano and adobo sauce and cook for 2 minutes more.

Add the pinto beans, kidney beans, beef broth, diced tomatoes with their juice, green chilies and tomato sauce. Reduce the heat to low and simmer for 1 hour. Taste the chili and adjust the seasonings.

Serve the chili in warm bowls topped with the shredded cheese and a dollop of sour cream.

SKILLET CORNBREAD with CHIPOTLE BUTTER Serves 8

This cornbread acquires a delicious crust from baking it in a cast iron skillet. The chipotle butter is delicious spread on the hot cornbread or on grilled corn, grilled fish, fresh vegetables or a grilled steak.

1 cup yellow cornmeal	2 large eggs, beaten
1 cup all-purpose flour	1 cup buttermilk
1/4 cup granulated sugar	1/4 cup vegetable oil
1 tablespoon baking powder	1 cup corn kernels, fresh or frozen and thawed
1/2 teaspoon salt	4 green onions, chopped

Preheat the oven to 400°F. Place a 10-inch cast iron skillet in the oven to heat.

In a mixing bowl, combine the cornmeal, flour, sugar, baking powder and salt. In a separate bowl, whisk together the eggs, buttermilk, oil, corn and green onions. Gently fold the wet ingredients into the dry ingredients, just until the mixture forms a batter.

Carefully remove the hot cast iron skillet from the oven, add the oil and swirl to coat the pan. Pour the batter into the hot skillet. Bake for 20-25 minutes or until the cornbread is golden brown and springs back to the touch.

Cut into wedges and serve.

CHIPOTLE BUTTER Makes 1 cup

2 sticks (8 ounces) unsalted butter, softened at room temperature
1 canned chipotle pepper in adobo sauce, pureed
Juice of 1 lime
Salt, to taste

Plcae the chipotle pepper in the bowl of a food processor and puree until smooth. Add the softened butter, lime juice and salt and blend well. Serve immediately or refrigerate and bring to room temperature before using.

GROWN-UP RICE KRISPY TREATS Makes 18 small triangles

This traditional American treat is made better with liqueur! Our adult version incorporates Grand Marnier, Amaretto, Crème de Menthe or your favorite liqueur (Oh...the possibilities are endless!). Dip the Treats in bittersweet chocolate, drizzle with caramel and serve with raspberry sauce or a cherry compote for a truly fun dessert.

1 stick (4 ounces) unsalted butter

10 ounces mini marshmallows

1/4 Grand Marnier (or your favorite liqueur)

1/2 teaspoon orange extract (use Vanilla or Almond extract as a
   substitute, depending upon your liqueur choice)

Pinch salt

6 cups crispy rice cereal

8 ounces bittersweet chocolate, melted

Melt the butter in a large saucepot over medium heat. Add the marshmallows, Grand Marnier, orange extract and salt. Stir until melted. Stir in the rice cereal to coat, then quickly pour into a 8"x8" greased baking pan. Press the mixture down using a spatula and let the treats cool to set.

Cut into triangles and dip one half of each treat into the melted chocolate. Refrigerate to set the chocolate.

Dinner For Two

SPINACH AND PEAR SALAD WITH WARM BACON DRESSING

SALMON PAPILLOTES WITH FENNEL AND OLIVES

DARK CHOCOLATE SOUFFLÉS

CAFÉ CACAO

SPINACH and PEAR SALAD
with WARM BACON DRESSING Serves 2

This warm salad always garners rave reviews. The bacon drippings add extra flavor and some crumbled blue cheese and toasted walnuts give it a nice finish. For a simple, hearty meal serve the salad with a delicious bowl of soup and Parmesan toasts.

4 slices bacon, diced

2 tablespoons extra-virgin olive oil

1 small shallot, minced

2 tablespoons red wine vinegar

1/2 teaspoon Dijon mustard

Freshly ground black pepper

3 cups fresh baby spinach leaves, washed and dried

1 pear, halved, seeded and sliced

1/4 cup dried cranberries

1/4 cup red onion, thinly sliced

Garnish: Crumbled blue cheese

Toasted walnuts

In a large skillet, cook the bacon over medium heat until crisp, then transfer it to paper towels to drain and reserve the rendered bacon fat. Pour 1/4 cup of the bacon fat back into the pan and add the olive oil and minced shallot. Sauté the shallot for 1 minute, then add the vinegar and Dijon and whisk to combine. Season with pepper to taste.

Combine the spinach, pears, cranberries and onion in a large salad bowl. Add the warm dressing and toss to coat. Top the salad with the crisp bacon, blue cheese and walnuts and serve immediately.

CHEF'S TIP:
Try using thick cut or apple-wood bacon for richer flavor.

SALMON PAPILLOTES
with FENNEL and OLIVES Serves 2

When you bake salmon in parchment paper (the French tern is "en Papillote"), the juices, flavor and aromas are trapped in a pretty package just waiting to escape. I'm a huge fan of fennel because of its distinctive flavor and I love the way it compliments the fish. An impressive presentation with a simple preparation, this dish is elegant enough for a dinner party but simple enough for a mid-week meal.

1 large fennel bulb, trimmed	3 tablespoons extra-virgin olive oil
1/4 cup Kalamata olives, pitted and halved	2 (6-ounce) salmon fillets, skinned
4 small red potatoes, cooked until tender and cut in half	2 tablespoons unsalted butter
2 teaspoons freshly grated lemon zest	6 lemon slices, cut very thin
4 fresh thyme sprigs	2 tablespoons dry white wine
1 large garlic clove, minced	Salt & freshly ground pepper
	2 parchment paper squares, each about 15-inches long

Preheat the oven to 400°F.

Halve the fennel bulb lengthwise and cut out the core. Using a mandoline or sharp knife, thinly slice the fennel lengthwise. In a large mixing bowl, toss the fennel, olives, potatoes, lemon zest, thyme sprigs and garlic with 2 tablespoons of the olive oil and season with salt and pepper.

Divide the fennel mixture among the centers of the parchment squares. Season the salmon fillets with salt and pepper and place each fillet on top of the fennel mixture. Top each fillet with a tablespoon of butter and 3 lemon slices and pour a tablespoon of the white wine into each papillote.

SALMON PAPILLOTES
with FENNEL and OLIVES continued

Working with one parchment square at a time, fold the left half of the paper over the salmon. Starting at one corner, fold the edge of the paper over in a triangle, about 1-inch at a time, following a semicircular around the salmon. Each fold should overlap the previous one until the papillote is completely sealed.

Place the packages directly on a baking sheet in the oven and bake for
20 minutes.

Remove the packages from the oven, place them on individual dinner plates and serve immediately, opening the packets at the table. To open the papillotes, cut an X into the top of each package, pulling the paper back to expose the fish.

DARK CHOCOLATE SOUFFLÉS Serves 2 (with one extra soufflé for good measure!)

The brilliance of this soufflé recipe is that it can be made several hours in advance and kept in the refrigerator until just before baking. Or, the soufflés can rest at room temperature for up to a half hour before baking, with no effect on the cooking time. If refrigerated, add an additional two minutes to the baking time.

1 tablespoon unsalted butter, softened

6 ounces high-quality bittersweet chocolate, chopped

   (I prefer Valrhona, Scharffenberger or Callebaut)

2/3 cup whole milk

1/2 tablespoon cornstarch

2 large egg yolks, at room temperature, lightly beaten

3 large egg whites, at room temperature

1/4 cup granulated sugar, plus more for the ramekins

Garnish: Whipped Cream

Preheat the oven to 375°F. Butter and sugar three 6-ounce ramekins. Place them on a rimmed baking sheet and set aside.

In a double boiler, melt the chocolate until smooth. Or, melt the chocolate in the microwave on 50% power, in 30-second increments, until melted. Let the chocolate cool.

In a medium saucepan, combine the milk and the cornstarch. Bring the mixture to a boil over medium heat, stirring constantly. Once the mixture comes to a simmer, cook 1 minute longer, or until thickened. Stir the melted chocolate into the milk mixture, then set it aside to cool slightly. Once cool, add the egg yolks and stir until well combined.

Using an electric mixer, whip the egg whites on medium speed until foamy. Slowly add the sugar and increase the speed to high. Whip until stiff peaks form.

Using a large rubber spatula, add one-third of the stiffly-beaten egg whites to the chocolate mixture and stir to combine. Add the next third of the beaten egg whites and gently fold the egg whites in. Add the remaining beaten egg whites and gently fold them in, until fully incorporated.

Spoon the mixture into the prepared soufflé ramekins; the mixture should come up to the top of each ramekin. Transfer the filled soufflé ramekins to the baking sheet and carefully place in the preheated oven. Bake until risen and just cooked through, about 15 minutes. Dust the top of each soufflé with powdered sugar and serve immediately, passing whipped cream at the table.

CAFÉ CACAO Serves 2

The natural affinity between coffee and chocolate is simply wonderful. Costa Rican or French roast are full-flavored and robust and the best choices for this blend. Roasted chicory root and the vanilla bean bind all the flavors together.

1/2 pound Costa Rican Coffee - whole bean

2 ounces Chicory

2 ounces Cocoa Nibs

1 Vanilla Bean

Grind together the coffee, chicory and nibs. Split the vanilla bean down the middle and cut it into 4 pieces. Add the vanilla bean to the coffee mixture. Brew in the normal brewing method.   Serve hot or iced. Store leftover Café Cacao in the refrigerator.

CHEF'S TIP:

For a spiked version, add 1 ounce of Kahlua, Sambuca or Brandy to each cup.

It's A Housewarming Party!

JAMIE'S FAVORITE LEMON DROP MARTINI

HOMEMADE SWEET AND SOUR MIX

CHICKEN WITH MARSALA, MUSHROOMS AND GORGONZOLA

SALMON WITH SPINACH EN CROUTE

ASPARAGUS WITH A HAZELNUT VINAIGRETTE

ROASTED POTATOES AND FENNEL WITH THYME & GARLIC

ROSEMARY FENNEL BREADSTICKS

CHOCOLATE COCONUT CREAM FONDUE

Jamie's Favorite LEMON DROP MARTINI Makes 12 Martinis

When it comes to serving drinks at a party, we plan cocktails that can be prepared in pitchers. This luscious Lemon Drop recipe can be mixed, without the ice, long before the party starts. Refrigerate the mixture until ready to serve, then have each guest shake their own Martini or pour the Lemon Drops over ice, for an "on-the-rocks" version.

3 cups Lemon flavored Vodka
1 1/2 cups Homemade Sweet & Sour Mix (recipe follows)
3/4 cup Cointreau

Combine the ingredients with ice in a martini shaker. Shake well and pour into sugar-rimmed martini glasses. Garnish each martini with a lemon wheel.

HOMEMADE SWEET AND SOUR MIX Makes 4 cups

Ideal for all your summer cocktails! For a twist, add fresh raspberries to the sugar/water mixture, then strain before you let it cool. Perfect for Iced Tea and vodka drinks too!

2 cups granulated sugar
1 cup water
1 cup fresh lemon juice
1 cup fresh lime juice

Combine water and sugar in a large saucepan. Stir over medium heat until sugar dissolves. Bring to a boil, then remove from the heat and let the syrup cool completely.

Combine the simple syrup, lemon juice and lime juice. Chill until cold. Store in the refrigerator for up to 1 week.

CHICKEN with MARSALA, MUSHROOMS and GORGONZOLA Serves 12

If you can't find Gorgonzola - a fine blue-veined Italian cheese made from cow's milk - use Roquefort or Stilton or the best blue cheese you can find.

6 boneless skinless chicken breasts, cut in half

Salt and freshly ground black pepper

8 tablespoons extra-virgin olive oil

3 cups cremini or white button mushrooms, sliced

2 large garlic cloves, minced

1/2 cup dry Marsala wine

1/3 cup heavy whipping cream

1/2 cup crumbled gorgonzola cheese

1/4 cup chopped fresh parsley

Season the chicken generously with salt and pepper.

In a large sauté pan, heat 3 tablespoons of the olive oil over medium-high heat. Sauté the chicken in two batches, turning once, until golden brown and just cooked through, about 3 minutes per side. Transfer the chicken to a plate and cover with foil to keep warm.

Return the pan to high heat and add the remaining 2 tablespoons of olive oil to the pan. Add the mushrooms and sauté until golden (before adding the salt!), about 4 minutes. Once the mushrooms are caramelized, season with salt and pepper. Reduce the heat to medium, add the garlic, and sauté one minute more.

Add the Marsala to the pan and deglaze, scraping up any browned bits from the bottom of the pan. Simmer until the Marsala is reduced slightly, about 2 minutes.

Stir in the cream and simmer (do not boil) until the sauce thickens slightly, about 3 minutes. Add two-thirds of the Gorgonzola cheese and stir until melted. Taste the sauce and adjust the seasoning.

Add the chicken to the sauce, along with any juices from the holding plate, and coat well. Serve from a chafing dish or warmer, garnished with the remaining Gorgonzola cheese and parsley.

CHEF'S TIP:

Always season mushrooms after sautéing! A smoking hot pan will allow the mushrooms to caramelize and acquire a wonderful rich flavor and aroma. If your pan is not hot enough or if you season right away, the liquid from the mushrooms leaches out and leaves you with soggy and flavorless mushrooms!

SALMON with SPINACH en CROUTE

Makes 2 Salmon en Croute and Serves 10 to 12

This is a great entertaining dish...Relatively easy, with a beautiful presentation that's always impressive. I love the fact that so much of it can be done in advance... assemble the salmon in the puff pastry the day before or the morning of and refrigerate until ready to bake.

2 tablespoons olive oil
1 small yellow onion, diced
1 fennel bulb, tops removed and diced
2 garlic cloves, minced
2 (10-ounce) packages frozen chopped spinach, thawed & squeezed dry
Salt & freshly ground pepper
1 box frozen puff pastry, thawed
1 (3-pound) salmon fillet, skinned & cut in half lengthwise
4 teaspoons freshly grated lemon zest
1 bunch chopped fresh dill
1 large egg
2 teaspoons milk

Heat the olive oil in a large sauté pan over medium heat. Add the onion and fennel and sauté until tender, about 8 minutes. Add the garlic and sauté 1 minute more. Add the spinach and salt and pepper to taste and cook for 5 minutes to heat through. Cool completely before using.

Lightly flour a large work surface and place one of the puff pastry sheets on the floured surface. Carefully unfold the puff pastry sheet, and using a rolling pin, just slightly roll it out, to smooth out any creases. Place the pastry sheet on a floured cookie sheet and store in the fridge. Repeat with the remaining sheet of puff pastry.

To assemble, beat the egg and milk together and set aside. Place one of the chilled puff pastry sheets on the work surface, with the long side facing you. Spread half of the spinach mixture over the pastry, leaving a 1-inch border around all sides of the puff pastry. Lay one of the salmon fillets on top of the spinach mixture, to cover the bottom half of the puff pastry sheet. Season the salmon with salt and pepper and sprinkle half of the lemon zest and a couple of teaspoons of the chopped dill over the top of the salmon. Using a pastry brush, brush the beaten egg mixture onto the edges of the pastry. Carefully fold the top of the puff pastry toward you, to encompass the salmon, and press the edges together, on all three sides, using the tines of a fork. Transfer the Salmon en Croute to a silpat or parchment-lined baking sheet and refrigerate until ready to bake. Repeat with the remaining ingredients.

When ready to bake, preheat the oven to 450°F. Cut a steam hole in the top of the pastry and brush the entire pastry with the remaining egg wash.

Bake for 15 minutes, then reduce the oven temperature to 350°F and bake an additional 15 minutes or until the pastry is puffed and golden all over.
Remove from the oven and let rest for 15 minutes before slicing and serving.

ROASTED POTATOES and FENNEL with THYME & GARLIC Serves 8

3 fennel bulbs

2 pounds small red potatoes, cut in half

1 garlic bulb, divided into peeled cloves

1 bunch fresh thyme

1/4 cup extra-virgin olive oil

Salt & freshly ground pepper

1/4 cup chopped fresh parsley

Preheat the oven to 425°F. Trim the fennel bulbs to remove their tops, keeping the root end intact, to hold the bulb together. Cut each fennel bulb into eight wedges.

Combine the fennel wedges, potatoes and thyme sprigs in a large roasting pan, toss with the olive oil and season with salt and pepper. Roast the vegetables for 40 to 45 minutes, tossing twice during the cooking process, or until tender and golden brown. Transfer to a warm platter and garnish with the chopped parsley.

ASPARAGUS with a HAZELNUT VINAIGRETTE Serves 8

This side dish is quick and simple and tastes "fancy" anytime you make it. Use diced sweet onion and toasted walnuts in place of the shallot and hazelnuts for an easy change of taste...A wonderful make ahead dish.

2 tablespoons Dijon mustard

3 tablespoons fresh lemon juice

1 large shallot, minced

6 fresh basil leaves, cut into thin strips

1 tablespoon fresh thyme leaves, minced

3 tablespoons fresh parsley, chopped

1/3 cup red wine vinegar

1/4 cup extra-virgin olive oil

1/4 cup Hazelnuts – toasted and chopped

Salt & freshly ground pepper

2 bunches asparagus

For the Vinaigrette, combine the mustard, lemon juice, shallot, basil, thyme, parsley and vinegar in a mixing bowl. Slowly add the oil, whisking constantly to create an emulsified dressing. Stir in the hazelnuts. Season to taste with salt and pepper.

Cut the tough base portion of the asparagus spears off and discard. Blanch the asparagus in boiling salted water until crisp-tender. Remove the asparagus from the boiling water and quickly drop the spears into a bowl of ice water to stop the cooking process. Drain the asparagus, dry them well and place them on a platter. Spoon the vinaigrette over the asparagus and serve warm or cold.

ROSEMARY FENNEL BREADSTICKS Makes 24 Breadsticks

Frozen bread dough makes these breadsticks simple to prepare and a
wonderful "homemade" compliment to your Housewarming Party.

1/4 cup grated Parmesan cheese

2 tablespoons dried rosemary leaves, crumbled

2 tablespoons dried fennel seeds, crushed

1 teaspoon kosher salt

1 teaspoon freshly ground black pepper

12 frozen Bridgford white rolls, thawed

1/4 cup unsalted butter, melted

In a small bowl combine the Parmesan cheese, rosemary, fennel seeds, salt and
pepper.

Cut each thawed roll in half. On a lightly floured surface and with floured hands,
roll each piece of dough into a rope, approximately 6 to 8-inches long. Place the
breadsticks on a greased cookie sheet, 2-3-inches apart. Using a pastry brush,
brush each breadstick with melted butter and sprinkle the surface of each breadstick with the cheese mixture, pressing the mixture in to stick.

Let the breadsticks rise until doubled in size.

Bake the breadsticks at 375°F for 10-15 minutes, or until golden brown.
Remove the breadsticks from the pan and allow them to cool on wire rack.

CHOCOLATE COCONUT CREAM FONDUE Serves 8

Our good friend Christy loves this recipe so much that she makes it all the time for her adorable daughters as a special treat. It tastes just like a melted mounds bar and is heavenly with frozen cheesecake squares for dipping!

1 (15 ounce) can cream of coconut (Coco Lopez)

12 ounces high-quality bittersweet chocolate, chopped
   (I prefer Valrhona, Scharffenberger or Callebaut)

1/3 cup heavy whipping cream

1/4 teaspoon coconut extract

For Dipping:

Frozen squares of Cheesecake

Cubes of Pound Cake

Biscotti or assorted Cookies

Strawberries

Pineapple chunks

Banana pieces

Marshmallows

Combine the cream of coconut and chocolate in a saucepan and stir the mixture over very low heat until smooth. Stir in the heavy cream and coconut extract.

Transfer the mixture to a fondue pot or double boiler. Serve with cookies, fresh fruit or any of the above ideas for dipping.

CHEF'S TIP:

You can easily prepare this recipe ahead of time, since it reheats beautifully. Prepare the mixture, cover it with plastic wrap and hold it at room temperature until ready to re-warm. It is best not to refrigerate the fondue, as it tends to separate.

GUYS NIGHT IN

BEER COCKTAILS

~~~

SOUTHERN SPICED NUTS

~~~

SALT AND PEPPER CRUSTED STEAKS

~~~

TOTALLY AMAZING SIRLOIN AND BRISKET BURGERS

~~~

GARLIC STEAK FRIES WITH GORGONZOLA CREAM SAUCE

~~~

THE ULTIMATE CHOCOLATE BROWNIE SUNDAE CAKE

BEER COCKTAILS Makes 6 Beer Cocktails

Beer cocktails are catching on! Have "the guys" try this potent beer blend.

6 lager beers

3 lemons, cut in half

Soy Sauce

Tabasco Sauce

Worcestershire sauce

6 Shots of Tequila

Pour each beer into a glass filled with ice and add the juice of half a lemon, a dash of soy, a dash of Tabasco and a dash of Worcestershire. Pour a shot of tequila into each glass. Stir and drink.

SOUTHERN SPICED NUTS Makes 6 Cups

This essential party snack is something to celebrate! You can substitute your favorite combination of nuts and add raisins, dried cranberries or wasabi peas for a fun twist.

4 tablespoons unsalted butter, melted

2 cups dry-roasted unsalted peanuts

2 cups pecan halves

2 cups whole almonds

2 tablespoons Worcestershire Sauce

2 teaspoons chipotle or ancho chili powder

1/2 teaspoon cayenne pepper

Salt to taste

Preheat the oven to 325ºF. In a large mixing bowl combine all of the ingredients and toss well. Spread the mixture in an even layer on a baking sheet and roast until the nuts are toasted, stirring often, about 20 minutes. Let cool and serve.

SALT and PEPPER CRUSTED STEAKS Serves 4

This restaurant method for cooking steaks produces a crisp crust that locks in the flavor and the juices and creates a perfectly cooked interior. Serve the steak with my Roasted Cherry Tomatoes and Garlic Steak Fries for a meal that can't be beat!

4 rib eye steaks

Kosher salt and freshly ground black pepper

2 tablespoons olive oil

Preheat the oven to 425°F. In a large ovenproof sauté pan, heat the olive oil over high heat until almost smoking. Liberally season the steaks with kosher salt and freshly ground black pepper. Add the steaks to the pan and brown them well on 1 side, about 2 minutes. Turn the steaks over and immediately place the pan in the oven to continue cooking.

A 2-inch steak will take approximately 8 minutes in the oven for medium-rare. (The time will vary depending on your oven calibration, how you like your steaks cooked and how thick they are.) Remove the steaks from the oven, remove them from the pan and allow them to rest for 5 minutes before serving.

ROASTED CHERRY TOMATOES

2 pints cherry tomatoes
Extra-virgin olive oil
salt and pepper

Preheat the oven to 425°F. Toss the tomatoes with olive oil, salt and pepper and place them in a casserole dish in a single layer. Roast for 10 minutes, or until the tomatoes have burst. Serve hot or at room temperature.

TOTALLY AMAZING SIRLOIN and BRISKET BURGERS Serves 6

Here's the low-down on having a killer Guys Night. Pick a theme and plan
a menu around it...Have a Sports Night, Movie Night, Music Night or Poker Night.
And, be sure to include this burger! The combination of sirloin and
brisket produces a fantastically tasty burger.

1 pound sirloin, ground twice

1 pound brisket, ground twice

Salt & freshly ground pepper

8 Kaiser buns, split

8 thin slices Fontina or cheddar cheese

For Garnish: Lettuce, tomato, onion, ketchup, mayonnaise, mustard

Preheat the barbecue or stove-top grill.

Combine the ground meat in a large mixing bowl and season with salt
and pepper. Gently mix the meat together, do not overmix. Shape into 6
one-third pound patties.

When the grill is hot, place the burgers on the grill and cook to the desired doneness (about 6 minutes per side for medium-rare). Top the burgers with
your cheese of choice during the last 2 minutes of grilling.   Place the buns on
the grill, cut side down, for 1 minute, to lightly toast them. Serve with the traditional garnishes.

GARLIC STEAK FRIES with GORGONZOLA CREAM SAUCE

This garlicky variation on steak fries served with a warm cheesy sauce is simply sensational. For a great shortcut, use frozen steak fries.

>**4 russet potatoes, each cut lengthwise into 8 wedges**
>**1/4 cup extra-virgin olive oil**
>**Salt & freshly ground pepper**
>**2 large garlic cloves, minced**
>**1/4 cup freshly grated Parmesan cheese**
>**2 tablespoons chopped fresh parsley**

Preheat the oven to 400°F. Once the oven has come to temperature, preheat a baking sheet in the oven for at least 5 minutes.

Toss the potato wedges with the olive oil and salt and pepper in a large mixing bowl. Spread the seasoned wedges in a single layer on the hot baking sheet. Roast the potatoes for 30 minutes, shaking the pan often. At the 30 minute mark, add the chopped garlic to the potatoes and roast 10 minutes more or until the potatoes are tender, golden and crispy. Toss the fries with the parmesan cheese and parsley and serve with the Gorgonzola Sauce for dipping.

GORGONZOLA CREAM SAUCE Makes about 1 1/2 Cups

>**4 cups heavy whipping cream**
>**4 ounces crumbly Gorgonzola (not creamy or "dolce")**
>**3 tablespoons freshly grated Parmesan cheese**
>**Freshly ground pepper**
>**3 tablespoons chopped fresh parsley**

Bring the heavy cream to a full boil in a medium saucepan over medium-high heat, reduce the heat to medium and steadily simmer the cream for 30 minutes, or until reduced by at least one-half or until it coats the back of a spoon. You can prepare the cream up to this point in advance, then bring it back to a boil and complete the recipe just before serving.

Remove the pot from the heat, add the Gorgonzola, Parmesan, salt, pepper and parsley and whisk rapidly until the cheeses melt. Serve immediately.

THE ULTIMATE
CHOCOLATE BROWNIE SUNDAE CAKE Serves 8

"Scrumptious" does not begin to describe this cake-like and fudgie dessert. When you layer coffee ice cream and caramel sauce in between the brownie layers, then freeze the cake and top with mounds of whipped cream and toasted pecans, you get the ultimate dessert!

8 (1 ounce) squares of unsweetened chocolate

2 sticks (8 ounces) unsalted butter

5 large eggs

3 cups granulated sugar

1 tablespoon pure vanilla extract

Pinch of salt

11/2 cups all-purpose flour

2 cups chopped pecans or walnuts, toasted

1 quart Ice Cream (your flavor of choice)

1 cup caramel sauce

Preheat the oven to 375°F. Generously grease two 9-inch cake pans.

Combine the chocolate and butter in the top of a double boiler over medium heat until completely melted. Or, combine the chocolate and butter in a large mixing bowl and microwave on 50% power, in 30-second increments, until melted. Let the mixture cool.

Using an electric mixer, beat the eggs, sugar, vanilla and salt on high speed for 10 minutes. Add the cooled chocolate mixture and mix well. Add the flour and blend just until combined.

THE ULTIMATE
CHOCOLATE BROWNIE SUNDAE CAKE continued

Stir in the nuts by hand and pour the batter into the prepared pans. Bake the brownie "cakes" for 40 minutes, then cool completely before removing from the pans.

Carefully remove the whole brownie "cakes" from the cake pans. Place one of the brownie layers on a flat plate (that fits in your freezer). Using a rubber spatula, quickly spread the ice cream onto the brownie. Top with the caramel sauce. Cover the ice cream with the other brownie layer and freeze for at least 4 hours or overnight.

To serve, remove the cake from the freezer 15 minutes before serving. Cut the brownie cake into slices and serve.

A Mexican Fiesta

MARGARITAS FOR A CROWD

GREEN CHILE CHEESE PUFFS

CHILLED AVOCADO AND PINEAPPLE SOUP WITH CHIPOTLE CREAM

GRILLED SALMON WITH JALAPEÑO HOLLANDAISE

CHICKEN ENCHILADAS WITH 4 CHEESES

CHOCOLATE CHILE CAKE

MARGARITAS FOR A CROWD Serves 8

Blended or stirred, this margarita recipe will please a crowd...and quickly!
The beauty of this classic drink is in the balance of tequila, lime juice and
orange liqueur.

1 cup freshly squeezed lime juice (about 8 to 10 limes)

1/4 cup superfine granulated sugar

1 cup Triple Sec

2 cups Gold Tequila

Ice Cubes

1 lime, cut in half

Coarse Sea Salt

Combine the lime juice, sugar, Triple Sec, Tequila and two big handfuls of
ice in a pitcher or blender.   Blend or stir to combine. If desired, rub the rims
of 8 glasses with the cut lime, then press the rims of the glasses into a plate
of salt. Pour the margaritas into the glasses and serve.

GREEN CHILE CHEESE PUFFS   Makes about 2 Dozen Cheese Puffs

The perfect appetizer to kick-off the festivities. Called gougères in French, these cocktail snacks are irresistible.

> 3/4 cup whole milk
>
> 5 tablespoons unsalted butter, cut into small pieces
>
> 1/2 teaspoon salt
>
> 3/4 cup all-purpose flour
>
> Pinch cayenne pepper
>
> 3 large eggs
>
> 1/4 cup chopped green chilies
>
> 1 cup grated Jack cheese
>
> 1/2 cup grated Parmesan cheese
>
> 1 egg, beaten with 1 teaspoon water – for the egg wash

Preheat the oven to 400°F. Line 2 baking sheets with parchment paper or silicone baking mats.

Combine the milk and butter in a saucepan and bring to a boil over medium heat. Combine the salt, flour and cayenne in a small bowl. As soon as the milk mixture boils, remove it from the heat and add the flour mixture. Place the pan back on the heat and cook for about 1 minute, stirring with a wooden spoon, until the mixture thickens and pulls away from the sides. Place the hot mixture into the bowl of a food processor fitted with the steel blade. Immediately add the eggs, jack cheese and Parmesan and pulse until the eggs are incorporated and the dough is smooth and thick. Stir in the diced chilies.

Spoon the mixture into a pastry bag fitted with a large plain round tip. Pipe mounds 1-inch wide and 1-inch high onto the baking sheets. With a wet finger, lightly press down the swirl at the top of each puff. (You can also use 2 spoons to scoop out the mixture and shape the puffs with damp fingers.) Brush the top of each puff lightly with the egg wash. Bake the puffs until golden brown, about 15 to 20 minutes. Serve immediately.

CHEF'S TIP:
To simulate a pastry bag, use a sealable plastic bag and snip off one corner with a scissor.

CHILLED AVOCADO and PINEAPPLE SOUP with CHIPOTLE CREAM Serves 6

Sweet and spicy, this soup makes the perfect start to a meal. I love the combination of the smooth, rich avocado and the tangy, sweet pineapple. Topped with the spicy crema, it's sure to be a hit!

3 ripe avocados, peeled and diced

3 cups pineapple chunks, fresh or canned and drained

Juice of 1 Lime

1/2 teaspoon chili powder

1/2 teaspoon ground cumin

Salt to taste

For the Chipotle Cream:

1/2 cup Mexican Crema or sour cream

1/2 teaspoon adobo sauce (from a can of Chipotle Chiles in Adobo)

Combine the avocado, pineapple, lime juice, chili powder, cumin, and salt to taste in a food processor and blend until very smooth. Transfer the soup to a container and refrigerate until well-chilled.

In a small bowl, combine the crema or sour cream with the adobo sauce and stir to combine. (Add adobo sauce to taste.)

To serve, ladle the soup into chilled bowls. Top each bowl with a tablespoon of the Chipotle Cream and serve.

GRILLED SALMON with JALAPEÑO HOLLANDAISE Serves 8

You can grill, broil or roast the salmon for this recipe. Serve the salmon, with the luscious sauce, along with garlicky greens or grilled asparagus and roasted or mashed potatoes.

Eight (6 ounces) salmon filets, skin left on
Salt and pepper

For the Jalapeño Hollandaise:
4 each egg yolks
1 tablespoon heavy whipping cream
Juice of 1 lemon
1/2 teaspoon salt
1/2 jalapeno pepper, ribs and seeds removed (or more, to taste)
1/2 pound (2 sticks) unsalted butter, melted and kept hot

Season the salmon with salt and pepper to taste. Heat the barbeque or stove-top grill to medium-high heat. When the grill is ready, place the salmon skin side down on the grill and cook for 5 minutes (don't attempt to turn it over earlier or it will stick). Carefully turn the salmon over and cook 3 to 5 minutes more (depending on the thickness), or until cooked through.

To prepare the Hollandaise, combine the egg yolks, cream, lemon juice, salt and jalapeno in a blender. Cover and blend until frothy. With the blender running, slowly pour the hot melted butter into the egg mixture. The sauce will thicken as the butter blends with the egg yolks. Adjust the seasoning and serve immediately, or hold the sauce in a double boiler until ready to serve.

Place the grilled salmon on warm plates and top each filet with a few tablespoons of the Hollandaise.

CHICKEN ENCHILADAS with 4 CHEESES Serves 8

This recipe is made easy by doctoring a can of enchilada sauce and by using a store bought rotisserie chicken or even leftover chicken.   We serve the enchiladas with chopped tomatoes and pickled jalapenos over the top for flavor and color and a black bean, corn and avocado salad alongside.

2 tablespoons olive oil

1 medium yellow onion, diced

1 (16 ounce) can enchilada sauce

2 teaspoons adobo sauce, from a can of Chipotle Chiles in Adobo

4 cups cooked, shredded chicken

2 cups Mexican-style 4-cheese blend

16 corn tortillas

Salt & freshly ground pepper

Heat the oil in a large, shallow ovenproof sauté pan over medium heat. Add the onion, season with salt and pepper and sauté until tender, about 10 minutes. Stir in the enchilada sauce and adobo sauce. Simmer over medium heat 10 minutes to meld the flavors, stirring often. Adjust the seasonings and reduce the heat to low.

Combine the shredded chicken and 1 cup of the cheese in a mixing bowl

Preheat the oven to 375°F. Soften the tortillas by wrapping a stack of 5 at a time in a paper towel. Microwave on high for 30 seconds or until tortillas are warm. Repeat with the remaining tortillas in batches. Fill each tortilla with 3 tablespoons of the chicken/cheese mixture and roll up.

Pour 1/3 of the enchiladas sauce into a 13x9 baking dish. Arrange the enchiladas in one layer, seem side down. Cover the enchiladas with the remaining sauce and sprinkle the remaining cheese over the top.

Bake uncovered for 25 minutes or until the enchiladas are heated through and the cheese is melted.

CHOCOLATE CHILE CAKE Makes 1 Two-Layer Cake

If you like it spicy, use the New Mexico Chile and the cayenne pepper called for in this recipe; for a mellower flavor, see the Chef's Tip below. The Ganache is an all-purpose filling and frosting that pleases any chocoholic.

1 1/4 cups cake flour

1/2 cup unsweetened cocoa powder,
   plus more for dusting the pans

3 tablespoons New Mexico chile powder

1/8 teaspoon ground cayenne pepper (optional)

1 teaspoon baking soda

1/4 teaspoon baking powder

1/2 teaspoon salt

1 stick (4 ounces)
   unsalted butter, at room temperature

1 1/2 cups granulated sugar

3 large eggs

1 teaspoon pure vanilla extract

1/2 cup buttermilk

1/2 cup brewed coffee

Chocolate Ganache, recipe follows

Preheat the oven to 350°F. Lightly grease two 9-inch cake pans and dust them with cocoa powder, shaking out any excess.

Sift together the flour, cocoa powder, chile powder, cayenne, baking soda, baking powder and salt.

Combine the butter and sugar in the bowl of an electric mixer and beat on high speed for 30 seconds, or until well combined and smooth. Add the eggs, one at a time, beating well after each addition. Continue beating, scraping down the sides of the bowl, until light and fluffy, about 5 minutes more.

With the mixer on low, beat in one-third of the flour mixture. Add in the vanilla extract, half of the buttermilk and half of the coffee, then another third of the flour mixture. Beat in the remaining buttermilk and coffee, then end by adding the remaining flour mixture. Mix just until combined.

Spread the batter evenly in the prepared pans. Bake for 30 minutes or until the center of the cake springs back when pressed. Cool the cake layers in the pans on a wire rack. Invert each cake onto a plate and trim the tops flat with a serrated knife. Spread one-third of the Ganache over one cake layer. Flip the other layer on top and frost the top and sides of the cake with the remaining Ganache.

CHEF'S TIP:

For a sweeter, mellower chile flavor, try using dried ancho chile powder
in place of the New Mexico Chile Powder and eliminate the cayenne.

CHOCOLATE GANACHE Makes about 2 Cups

Chocolate ganache has multiple uses: Dip fresh or dried fruit in the ganache while it's still warm and place the fruit on a silicone mat or parchment paper lined cookie sheet to set. Use the ganache in it's semi-soft stage as a frosting (as used in the Chocolate Chile Cake recipe) or let the ganache firm up completely and form rounded teaspoons of the mixture, roll the balls in cocoa, and you have chocolate truffles.

12 ounces bittersweet chocolate, chopped

1 cup heavy whipping cream

Place the chocolate in a mixing bowl. In a small saucepan, heat the cream over medium heat to just before a simmer. Pour the hot cream over the chocolate. Gently stir until smooth. Let the Ganache sit until slightly thickened, about 10 minutes; it should be spreadable, but still pourable.

CHEF'S TIP:

If your Ganache doesn't have a shiny finish, try blending in a few drops of cold heavy cream to give it a great shine!

WINE TIP:

Port is a fortified wine from the Douro Valley in Portugal, where all authentic port is produced, and one of my favorite pairings with chocolate. Ruby Port, a less-sweet style, should be served around 65°F and sipped slowly for the ultimate enjoyment.

An Afternoon Tea Baby Shower

SMOKED TROUT MOUSSE

~~~

SALAD NICOISE

~~~

JULIANN'S STRAWBERRY SCONES

~~~

LEMON BLUEBERRY TEA BREAD

~~~

CHOCOLATE-RASPBERRY TRUFFLE CHEESECAKE

SMOKED TROUT MOUSSE Makes 1 1/2 Cups of Mousse

Serve this mousse atop cucumber rounds, black bread slices or
as a dip with crudités. Other smoked fish, including smoked Sturgeon
and Salmon are perfect substitutes.

8 ounces cream cheese, softened

3 tablespoons sour cream

4 ounces smoked trout

Juice and zest of 1 lemon

1 tablespoon chopped fresh dill

1 teaspoon prepared cream-style horseradish, or to taste

Salt & freshly ground pepper

Garnish: chopped fresh chives

Combine the cream cheese and sour cream in the bowl of a food processor and
blend until smooth. Add the remaining ingredients and pulse to combine.

Transfer the mousse to a serving bowl and refrigerate until cold.
Serve garnished with chopped chives.

SALAD NICOISE Serves 8

Fill a large platter with arugula and watercress and arrange the different components of this salad on top. The presentation is colorful and very impressive...
A French Classic at its best. Canned Tuna in water or olive oil can be substituted.

4 1-inch-thick fresh tuna steaks (about 2 pounds)

Extra-virgin olive oil

Salt & freshly ground pepper

3/4 pound French string beans (haricots verts),
   stems removed and blanched

1 recipe French Potato Salad

8 ripe roma tomatoes cut into wedges

4 hard-boiled eggs, peeled and cut in half

1/2 pound good black olives, pitted

1 bunch watercress or arugula

1 can anchovies (optional)

For the Vinaigrette:

1/2 cup Champagne vinegar

1 Dijon mustard

1 teaspoon anchovy paste

Salt & pepper, to taste

1 1/2 cups extra-virgin olive oil

To sear the tuna, heat a sauté pan or stove-top grill until very hot. Brush the fish with olive oil and season with salt and pepper. Grill each tuna steak for 1 1/2 to 2 minutes per side. The center should be raw but warm, or the tuna will be tough and dry. Arrange the tuna, haricots verts, potato salad, tomatoes, eggs, olives, and anchovies on top of the arugula or watercress on a large platter.

Meanwhile make the vinaigrette. Using a blender or mixing bowl, combine the vinegar, mustard, anchovy paste and salt pepper. Slowly drizzle in the olive oil to make a vinaigrette.

Use part of the vinaigrette in the French Potato Salad, then drizzle a bit of vinaigrette over the Nicoise platter and serve additional dressing on the side.

JULIANN'S STRAWBERRY SCONES <small>Makes 12 Scones</small>

We have the fondest memories of having Afternoon Tea in London...where the scones were flaky and delicious. The sweetness of the scones, combined with tangy clotted cream and homemade jam is always delightful. You can adapt this recipe with an endless array of additions to create your own signature Scones...tart cherries, chocolate chunks, finely chopped rosemary, dried apricots or candied ginger. We recommend that you freeze the raw formed scones before baking, as it helps keep their shape during baking...and it makes for easy advanced preparation. These scones are "pretty in pink", just like Juliann!

> **4 1/2 cups all-purpose flour or pastry flour**
>
> **1/2 cup granulated sugar, plus more for sprinkling the scones**
>
> **1 tablespoon plus 1 1/2 teaspoons baking powder**
>
> **1/2 teaspoon salt**
>
> **2 1/4 sticks (9 ounces) unsalted butter, cut into pieces and kept cold**
>
> **1 cup dried strawberries, chopped**
>
> **1 2/3 cups heavy whipping cream plus more for brushing the scones**

In a food processor, combine the flour, sugar, baking powder, salt and butter. Pulse the processor, to cut in the butter, until the butter is the size of small peas. Transfer the mixture to a mixing bowl and stir in the strawberries.

Add the cream to the flour mixture and incorporate with a spatula. With your hands, work the dough just until it comes together and all of the liquid is incorporated. (Don't overwork the dough...it should still be crumbly)

Turn the dough out onto a floured work surface. Press the dough together and flatten to 3/4-inch thick. Cut the dough into 12 scones using a 3-inch round cutter. Wrap the scones individually and freeze until ready to bake.

Preheat the oven to 350°F. Place the scones 2-inches apart on a baking sheet lined with parchment paper or a silicone mat. Brush the tops with cream and sprinkle sugar evenly over each scone. Bake until golden, about 30 to 35 minutes. Cool before removing from the baking sheet.

CHEF'S TIP:

Pastry flour can be found in health food stores or from mail order catalogs.
Use it for making flaky pie crusts, pastry and cookies. If pastry flour is unavailable,
substitute equal parts of all-purpose flour and cake flour combined.

LEMON BLUEBERRY TEA BREAD Makes 1 Loaf

This bread is moist and rich and lovely served at breakfast or with tea.
Make mini-loaves for holiday gifts or freeze the bread for up to 3 months.
To serve, decorate the top of the bread with ribbons of fresh lemon zest.

For the Bread:

2 large eggs

Zest and juice of 1 lemon

Pinch of salt

1 cup granulated sugar

1/3 cup crème fraiche or sour cream

1 1/4 cups all-purpose flour

2 1/2 teaspoons baking powder

4 tablespoons unsalted butter, melted

1 cup fresh or frozen blueberries

For the Lemon Glaze:

1 cup powdered sugar

Juice of 1 lemon

Preheat the oven to 350°F. Butter and flour a standard-sized loaf pan.

To make the bread, whisk together the eggs, lemon juice and zest, salt and granulated sugar in a large bowl. Stir in the crème fraiche, flour and baking powder, just until combined. Gently fold in the melted butter and blueberries and stir just until blended.

Pour the batter into the prepared pan. Bake the tea bread for 25 to 30 minutes, or until a cake tester inserted in the center of the loaf comes out clean. Allow the bread to cool in the pan for 5 minutes, then turn the bread out, drizzle with the glaze and allow to cool completely.

To make the lemon glaze, combine the powdered sugar and lemon juice and stir until smooth. Adjust the thickness of the frosting with a drop of water at a time, if necessary.

CHOCOLATE-RASPBERRY TRUFFLE CHEESECAKE Serves 12

This decadent cheesecake makes a beautiful centerpiece and is always receives rave reviews! Be sure to use a high-quality chocolate (such as Vahlrona, Callebaut or Scharffenberger) and add a splash of the Chambord to your whipped cream for an extra indulgence (it will keep the whipped cream fluffy for longer too...alcohol added during the whipping process does that!).

For the Crust:

1 (9 ounce) box chocolate wafer cookies

3 tablespoons granulated sugar

6 tablespoons unsalted butter, melted

For the Filling:

8 ounces bittersweet chocolate, chopped into pieces

1/4 cup hot strong coffee

24 ounces cream cheese, cut into cubes

1 cup sour cream

1 cup granulated sugar

2 large eggs

2 tablespoons heavy whipping cream

1 teaspoon pure vanilla extract

1/4 cup Chambord Liqueur (or other raspberry liqueur)

For Garnish:

Whipped cream, fresh raspberries, fresh mint sprigs

For the crust, combine the wafer cookies and sugar in a food processor and process to fine crumbs. Add the melted butter and process to combine. Press the mixture onto the bottom and 1-inch up the sides of a 9-inch springform pan. Set the pan aside.

Clean the bowl of the food processor and place the chopped chocolate in the processor. With the food processor running, pour the hot coffee through the chute. Blend until the chocolate is melted and smooth. Add the cream cheese and blend until smooth. Add the sour cream, sugar, eggs, cream, vanilla and Chambord and blend until the mixture is smooth.

Preheat the oven to 350°F. Pour the mixture into the prepared crust, and bake for 1 hour or until just set. (The center will still look slightly soft.) Let the cheesecake cool to room temperature then refrigerate for at least 8 hours.

To serve, garnish each slice with a dollop of whipped cream, a few fresh raspberries and a sprig of fresh mint.

A Grand Graduation Party

CARAMELIZED ONION DIP

~~~~~~

REUBEN DIP

~~~~~~

HOT CLAM DIP

~~~~~~

ANTIPASTO PLATTER

~~~~~~

GRILLED CORN ON THE COB with MAPLE CHIPOTLE GLAZE

~~~~~~

CHIPOTLE CORN CHOWDER

~~~~~~

DOUBLE LEMON BARS

CARAMELIZED ONION DIP Makes about 2 Cups

Better than any onion dip you've ever had...Sweet and creamy, and the real thing!
The secret to the caramelized flavor is to slowly cook the onions until golden
brown. Serve the dip with any kind of dipping chip, veggies or pretzels.

2 tablespoons extra-virgin olive oil

2 tablespoons unsalted butter

2 large yellow onions – peeled, cut in half and sliced thinly

Salt & white pepper

2 tablespoons dry white wine or chicken broth

1/2 cup sour cream

1/2 cup mayonnaise

4 ounces whipped cream cheese

Heat the oil and butter in a sauté pan over medium heat. Add the onions and
sauté, stirring often over medium heat for about 10 minutes. Season the onions
with salt and pepper and reduce the heat to low. Cook 20 minutes more or until
the onions are golden brown and caramelized. Increase the heat to medium and
add the wine to deglaze. Scrape up any bits from the bottom of the pan, then
remove the pan from the heat and let the onions cool to room temperature.

In a large mixing bowl, whip together the sour cream, mayonnaise and cream
cheese until smooth. Add the cooled caramelized onions and mix to blend well.
Adjust the seasoning and serve at room temperature.

REUBEN DIP Makes One 9-inch Pie Pan of Dip

Simply said, we love Reuben sandwiches.....so this is now our favorite dip!
Serve it with toasted cocktail rye bread for dipping.

8 ounces cream cheese, at room temperature

2 cups shredded Swiss cheese

1/2 cup Thousand Island salad dressing

1 cup corned beef, chopped

1/2 cup sauerkraut, rinsed and drained

1/4 cup grated Parmesan cheese

Preheat the oven to 375°F. Mix together the cream cheese and 1 cup of the Swiss cheese in a mixing bowl. Spread the mixture onto the bottom of a 9-inch pie plate. Drizzle with half of the salad dressing. Top with the corned beef, then top with the sauerkraut. Drizzle with the remaining salad dressing. Top with the remaining Swiss cheese and Parmesan cheese.

Bake for 20 to 25 minutes or until the dip begins to bubble and the cheese is melted.

HOT CLAM DIP Serves 8

Cut out the center of a round French bread and form chunks from the inside of the loaf. When ready to serve, pour the clam dip into the hollowed-out bread and serve with the bread chunks, for dipping. This is one of our favorite comfort foods and can be served either hot or cold.

2 (8 ounce) packages cream cheese, softened

2 tablespoons yellow onion, grated

2 teaspoons lemon juice

2 tablespoons beer

1 teaspoon Worcestershire sauce

1 teaspoon hot pepper sauce

3 (6.5 ounce) cans minced clams, drained

Preheat the oven to 350°F. In a mixing bowl combine the cream cheese, onion, beer, Worcestershire sauce, lemon juice and hot pepper sauce. Mix well, then fold the clams into the mixture. Pour the clam mixture into a shallow baking dish.

Bake for 20 minutes or until heated through.

Serve with sliced French bread, potato chips, corn chips or crackers.

ANTIPASTO PLATTER

Antipasto translates literally to "before the meal" and is the traditional start to every Italian feast. Since an antipasto looks and tastes so fabulous, I serve it at home as a casual meal or at the outset of many of my parties. There's no cooking required, which makes it a wonderfully relaxed starter.

Prosciutto, sliced thin

Genoa Salami, sliced thin

Spicy Sopressata, sliced thin

Provolone or Mozzarella cheese, sliced

Fontina cheese, sliced

Parmigiano Reggiano cheese, broken into chunks

Chunk white tuna, broken in bite-size chunks

Anchovy filets, rinsed and patted dry

Marinated mushrooms

Marinated artichokes

Marinated red peppers

An assortment of Olives (kalamata, nicoise, picholine)

Pepperoncini

Pickled cherry peppers

Roll the meats and cheeses into cigar or funnel shapes and arrange on a large serving platter. Pile the tuna chunks, anchovies, mushrooms, artichokes, red peppers, olives and hot peppers along the edges of the serving tray. (Think of arranging contrasting colors as you separate the items, to create a masterpiece!)

The platter can be prepared several hours ahead and refrigerated. Remove from the refrigerator 30 minutes before serving. Serve with focaccia or ciabatta bread slices.

GRILLED CORN ON THE COB
with MAPLE CHIPOTLE GLAZE Serves 8

The smoky heat of chipotles and the sweetness of maple syrup are absolutely divine when combined with the flavor of grilled corn.

Maple Chipotle Glaze:

Two to three canned chipotle chilies in adobo sauce

2/3 cup maple syrup

1/2 stick unsalted butter

1 whole garlic clove

Salt & freshly ground pepper

8 ears of corn, cleaned and husks pulled bac

Finely chop the chilies, using a food processor or by hand. Place the minced chilies in a small saucepan along with the maple syrup, butter and garlic. Season with salt and pepper to taste. Place the pan over medium heat and bring to a boil, stirring often. Reduce the heat to low and simmer for 10 minutes or until thickened. Skim any scum from the top of the glaze and discard it, then set the glaze aside.

Heat your barbecue or stovetop grill to medium heat. Rinse the cleaned ears of corn with water and place them directly on the grill. Grill, turning often, until tender and slightly charred in spots, about 10 minutes. Brush the corn with the glaze and continue to grill for about 5 minutes more. Serve immediately.

CHIPOTLE CORN CHOWDER Serves 8

This hearty chowder is the perfect addition to a buffet-style menu. The recipe is a two-step process... but well worth it. Use my Grilled Corn recipe (perfect for backyard barbeques!) to create flavorful kernels, then cut the corn off the cobs and proceed with the soup recipe. Keep the chowder hot on a small burner or in a crock pot on your buffet.

4 slices applewood smoked bacon, diced

2 tablespoons olive oil

1 yellow onion, diced

1 fennel bulb, trimmed and diced

1 red, orange or yellow bell pepper, seeded and diced

3 sprigs fresh thyme

1 bay leaf

8 ears corn, (grilled with the Maple Chipotle Glaze,
as directed above if desired), kernels cut off the cobs

4 cups lobster stock or chicken broth

11/2 cups half & half

Salt & freshly ground pepper

In a large soup pot, cook the bacon until crisp. Remove the bacon with a slotted spoon and set aside. Add the olive oil to the pot along with the onion and fennel and sauté for 10 minutes, or until tender. Add the bell pepper, thyme and bay leaf and sauté 2 minutes more. Add the stock or broth and bring to a simmer. Cook for 15 minutes to blend flavors, then add the corn and simmer 15 minutes more.

Remove the pot from the heat and stir in the half and half. Adjust the seasoning to taste. Place half of the chowder in the blender (working in batches) and puree until smooth. Add the pureed mixture back to the corn chowder.

To serve, ladle the chowder into warm bowls and top with a few pieces of the crispy bacon.

CHEF'S TIP:

Use vegetable stock in place of the lobster stock or chicken broth to make a delicious vegetarian chowder.

To impart extra flavor into your chowder, after cutting the kernels from the cobs, place the cobs in a large pot along with your broth of choice. Bring the liquid to a simmer and simmer 10 minutes to release the corn flavor from the cobs. Remove the cobs and discard, then proceed with the recipe, using the infused liquid.

DOUBLE LEMON BARS Makes 24 Bars

Lana, the co-author of this cookbook, my Mom, best friend and the best cook I know submitted this original recipe to Bon Appetit Magazine and it appeared in the "Too Busy to Cook" column in the July 1991 issue. Many reviewers claim it is "the best Lemon Bar they've ever had". One great cook said that she actually ate the whole pan by herself!

For the Crust:

1 1/2 cups all purpose flour

1/4 cup powdered sugar

1 tablespoon lemon zest, freshly grated

1 1/2 sticks unsalted butter, cut into pieces and kept cold

For the Filling:

4 large eggs

1 1/4 cups granulated sugar

1/2 cup fresh lemon juice

1 tablespoon plus 1 teaspoon all-purpose flour

1 tablespoon lemon zest, freshly grated

Garnish: Powdered sugar

Preheat the oven to 350°F. Combine the flour, powdered sugar and lemon zest in the bowl of a food processor. Add the butter and pulse the processor until the mixture resembles coarse meal. Press the mixture into the bottom of a 9x13x2-inch baking dish. Bake until golden brown, about 25 to 30 minutes. Remove from the oven and maintain the oven temperature.

Combine the eggs, sugar, lemon juice, flour and lemon zest in a mixing bowl. Whisk to combine, then pour into the baked crust. Bake until the mixture is set, about 20 to 30 minutes.

Cool the Lemon Bars completely then cut into 24 bars. Sift powdered sugar over the top of the bars before serving.

An Anniversary To Remember

A CHEESE BOARD FOR EVERY OCCASION

HORSERADISH-CRUSTED RIB EYE ROAST

CLASSIC POTATO GRATIN

ROASTED ROOT VEGETABLES with ROSEMARY and LEMON

BITTERSWEET CHOCOLATE TRUFFLES

A CHEESE BOARD
FOR EVERY OCCASION Serves 6 to 8

Whether you're serving cheese as a starter with cocktails, as a first course with salad, or to finish a meal, a well chosen cheese board is a simple, elegant and unique conversation piece.

CHOICES FOR THE CHEESE BOARD

I recommend you pick five or six good cheeses and pair them with savory and sweet accompaniments like candied nuts for a sweet and salty crunch, fresh pears or apples, fig paste, dried apricots or tart cherries. Infused honeys, such as Lavender Honey or Truffled Honey, are delicious drizzled over hard cheeses and paper-thin soft breads or crisp crackers pair well with a multitude of cheese choices. For your next Wine & Cheese Party, try serving a soft goat cheese, a creamy Camembert, a blue-veined cheese such as Gorgonzola and a hard cheese like Parmigiano Reggiano.

Set your cheeses on a large marble slab or cheese board and remember to bring them to room temperature an hour before your guests arrive (you can open the wine to breathe at the same time). Arrange the cheeses clockwise from the mildest to the strongest and pair wines accordingly or serve a sparkling wine for a universal compliment.

With so many wonderful varieties to choose from, serving the ultimate cheese course is a creative and colorful celebration every time. Experiment to find your favorite cheese!

continued

A CHEESE BOARD
FOR EVERY OCCASION continued

PAIRING CHEESE WITH WINE

Properly matching cheese and wine can enhance the overall flavor of both the wine and the cheese. You might choose your cheeses by country of origin, and serve wines from the region, such as a Spanish Rioja paired with Manchego (an aged sheep's milk cheese and the pride of Spain).

For another quick tip, try not to pair strong tastes together, such as a pungent cheese with a big, bold wine. Pair sweet wines with salty cheeses (such as Parmigiano Reggiano) or soft and elegant white wines with rich and creamy cheeses (such as a Triple Cream Brie).

Blue cheeses such as Gorgonzola or Stilton pair well with sweet dessert wines such as a Port or Ice Wine along with Madeira and Sherry. To accompany fresh cheeses like goat or feta, choose a Beaujolais Nouveau or a Vouvray. Soft-ripened cheeses like Brie or Camembert compliment Champagne perfectly! For aged cheeses like Cheddars try a Cabernet Sauvignon. For semi-soft cheeses, like Havarti, serve a Zinfandel.

HORSERADISH-CRUSTED RIB EYE ROAST Serves 8

A rib eye roast is a standing rib roast, also known as Prime Rib, without the bones. If there isn't a rib eye roast in the meat case at your local store, select a standing rib roast, then ask the butcher to cut off the bones (ask for the bones to take home). You can cook the ribs separately and enjoy them alone.....after the party!

1 (4 pound) Rib Eye Roast, tied with
   butcher's twine for even cooking

Salt & freshly ground pepper

2 tablespoons Extra-Virgin Olive Oil

1/4 cup Dijon mustard

2 cups fresh Horseradish, peeled and shredded

2 tablespoons fresh chopped parsley

1 teaspoon fresh chopped rosemary

1 teaspoon fresh chopped thyme

1 cup dry red wine

1 cup beef broth

4 tablespoons unsalted butter,
   cut into small cubes and kept chilled

Preheat the oven to 425°F. Season the roast with salt and pepper. In a large sauté pan heat the olive oil over high heat. Sear the meat until evenly browned on all sides. Remove from the heat.

Place a wire rack in the bottom of a roasting pan and place the roast on the rack. Spread the Dijon mustard on the top and sides of the roast. In a mixing bowl combine the shredded horseradish, parsley, rosemary and thyme. Season the mixture with salt and pepper. Using your hands, press the horseradish mixture evenly over the mustard on the top and sides of the roast.

Roast the meat at 425°F for 15 minutes. Reduce the oven temperature to 350°F and roast for an additional hour or until the roast registers 135°F on an instant-read thermometer or meat thermometer, for medium-rare meat (the meat will continue to rise in temperature about 5 to 10 degrees as it rests). Remove the roast from the oven and transfer the meat to a serving platter. Allow the meat to rest for 10 minutes before carving.

Meanwhile, place the roasting pan on top of the stove over low heat. Skim the fat from the pan, then add the red wine and deglaze the pan, scraping any brown bits of crust from the bottom of the pan. Add the beef broth and bring the mixture to a simmer. Allow the sauce to simmer until reduced by half, about 3 minutes. To finish the sauce, remove the pan from the heat and slowly whisk in the cold butter.

CHEF'S TIP:

The approximate cooking time for medium-rare meat is 18-22 minutes per pound. Remember that cooking times vary dependent upon your oven and the temperature of your roast when it enters the oven. For beef, an internal temperature registering 130°F is rare, 140°F is medium and well done registers 150°F.

CLASSIC POTATO GRATIN Serves 6 to 8

Wafer thin slices of potato are key to this satisfying side dish. You can use a mix of potatoes such as sweet potatoes, Peruvian purples or Yukon gold. This classic French potato gratin is the perfect complement to both fancy meals, like rack of lamb, and homey dishes like roast chicken or meatloaf. Try to buy a good-quality Gruyere or Emmenthaler, which will be moderately assertive yet mellow and nutty.

2 pounds Yukon Gold or russet potatoes, peeled

3 cups heavy whipping cream

Salt & freshly ground pepper

Pinch of freshly grated nutmeg

2 garlic cloves, peeled and smashed

3/4 cup finely shredded Gruyere or Emmenthaler cheese

1/4 cup shaved Grana Padano or Parmesan cheese

Heat the oven to 400°F. Using a very sharp knife or a mandolin, cut the potatoes into 1/8-inch slices.

Combine the potatoes, cream, salt, pepper, nutmeg and garlic in a large saucepan. Cook the mixture over medium heat until the cream boils, stirring occasionally. Gently shake the pan so as not to break up the potato slices.

When the cream boils, carefully slide the mixture into a buttered 3 quart baking dish. Discard the garlic cloves. Shake the dish a bit to let the slices settle, then sprinkle the surface with the Gruyere or Emmenthaler cheese and top with Grana Padano.

Bake until the potatoes are extremely tender when pierced with a knife and the surface is golden, about 45 minutes.

Let the Gratin cool for 10 minutes before serving.

ROASTED ROOT VEGETABLES
with ROSEMARY and LEMON Serves 8

Fall vegetables bring to mind hearty food, autumn colors, roasting and braising. Choose the root vegetables you like best, but remember that variety lends both complex flavor and appealing color to the mixture. The root vegetables also make a delicious puree.

**1 pound red skinned potatoes, scrubbed and
    cut in halves or quarters**
2 fennel bulbs, trimmed and cut into 2-inch pieces
1 pound carrots, peeled and cut into 1-inch pieces
1 pound parsnips, peeled and cut into 1-inch pieces
1 pound turnips, peeled and cut into 1-inch pieces
12 garlic cloves
4 sprigs fresh rosemary
1/4 cup extra-virgin olive oil
Salt & freshly ground pepper

Garnish:
4 tablespoons freshly grated lemon zest
1/4 cup chopped fresh parsley

Preheat the oven to 425°F.

In a large mixing bowl, combine the potatoes, fennel, carrots, parsnips, turnips, garlic cloves and rosemary sprigs. Drizzle with the olive oil and toss to coat. Season the vegetables generously with salt and pepper. Spread the root vegetables in a single layer onto two or three baking sheets.

Roast the vegetables for 1 hour, tossing every fifteen minutes during cooking, or until the vegetables are tender and golden brown.

Transfer the roasted vegetables to a large serving bowl, garnish with the lemon zest and chopped parsley and serve.

CHEF'S TIP:
You can prepare the Roasted Root Vegetables up to 4 hours ahead. Reheat them in a 450°F oven until heated through, about 15 minutes, before serving.

BITTERSWEET CHOCOLATE TRUFFLES Makes 24 Truffles

These heavenly chocolate morsels are some of the easiest you will ever make. They are especially delicious served with an espresso or a glass of Cabernet. The truffles will hold for at least 2 weeks in the refrigerator... dust them again with cocoa powder before serving.

8 ounces high quality bittersweet chocolate, chopped

(I prefer Valrhona, Scharffenberger or Callebaut)

1/2 cup heavy cream

1/2 cup sweetened condensed milk

2 tablespoons unsweetened cocoa powder

2 tablespoons unsalted butter

For Dusting: 1 cup unsweetened cocoa powder

Melt the chocolate in the top of a double boiler over medium heat until completely melted. Or, melt the chocolate in a mixing bowl in the microwave on 50% power in 30-second increments, until melted.

In a saucepan, combine the cream and condensed milk over low heat. Heat the mixture just until warm to the touch, do not simmer. Remove the saucepan from the heat and whisk in the melted chocolate, cocoa powder and butter.

Scrape the mixture into a small bowl, let cool to room temperature, then refrigerate until set, about 4 hours or overnight.

To form the truffles, scoop the cold chocolate mixture by the teaspoon and working quickly, roll into 1-inch balls. Set the truffles on a cookie sheet or large plate and refrigerate after forming to set.

To dust the truffles, place the cup of cocoa powder in a shallow bowl. Add the truffles, 6 or so at a time, and coat the truffles thoroughly with the cocoa, shaking off any excess.

Store the truffles in an airtight container in the refrigerator until ready to serve. Remove from the refrigerator 15 minutes before serving.

A Summer Celebration

GRILLED CORNBREAD SALAD with ARUGULA and FRESH HERBS

~~~~~

GREAT-ON-THE-GRILL BEER CAN CHICKEN

~~~~~

PIZZA ON THE GRILL

~~~~~

BUTTERFLIED LEG OF LAMB PROVENCAL

~~~~~

SIMPLE & SENSATIONAL STRAWBERRY CREAM PIE

GRILLED CORNBREAD SALAD
with ARUGULA and FRESH HERBS Serves 4

This casual salad, served with a glass of Sauvignon Blanc, makes a delicious first course. Simply add leftover chicken or sliced steak and use store-bought cornbread and it doubles as a delicious, simple weeknight meal. The addition of fresh herbs in their whole leaf form adds a wonderful bright flavor and aromatic element to the dish.

For the Vinaigrette:

1/4 cup red wine vinegar

1 tablespoon Dijon mustard

2/3 cup extra-virgin olive oil

Salt & freshly ground pepper

For the Salad:

1 (6 inch round) or 4 (3-inch) Squares Homemade or
 Store-bought Cornbread

Extra-virgin olive oil

1 head of radicchio, cut into quarters

1 medium red onion, cut into 1/2-inch-thick round slices

4 cups baby arugula leaves

1 cup cherry tomatoes, cut in half

1/2 seedless cucumber, thinly sliced

1/2 cup black or Nicoise olives

12 fresh basil leaves, torn into pieces

1/4 cup fresh mint leaves, left whole

1/4 cup fresh parsley leaves, left whole

For the vinaigrette, combine the vinegar and mustard in a blender and pulse to combine. With the blender running, slowly add the oil, in a thin stream, to form an emulsion. Season with salt and pepper to taste.

continued

GRILLED CORNBREAD SALAD
with ARUGULA and FRESH HERBS continued

For the salad, heat the barbeque or stove-top grill to high. Cut the cornbread into 1-inch wide strips and brush the cornbread strips lightly on all sides with the olive oil. Brush the onion slices and the radicchio quarters with olive oil as well and season with salt and pepper.

Grill the corn bread, just until grill marks appear, about 1 minute per side. Grill the onion slices until tender and golden, about 5 minutes per side. Grill the radicchio until just beginning to wilt, about 1 minute total.

Cut the grilled cornbread into 1-inch cubes and roughly chop the grilled onions. Combine the cornbread cubes and grilled onions with the remaining ingredients, add vinaigrette to taste, toss gently and serve.

GREAT-ON-THE-GRILL
BEER CAN CHICKEN Serves 4

A beer can serves as a vertical roasting rack for this moist, juicy and delicious barbecued chicken. You can cook the chicken in your oven or on the grill. The bubbling liquid adds a constant source of moisture to the chicken during the cooking process that keeps it from drying out....The skin gets crispy while the meat remains juicy; Perfect!

1 can (12 ounces) beer or peach nectar or cola

3 fresh rosemary sprigs

5 tablespoons of your favorite Spice Rub

1 whole chicken (about 3 1/2 pounds)

2 teaspoons extra-virgin olive oil

For Dipping: Your favorite BBQ Sauce

Open the can of beer, juice or soda, and drink half! Spoon one tablespoon of the Spice Rub into the can. Then, stuff the rosemary sprigs into the can and set the can aside.

Rinse the chicken, inside and out, under cold water, removing any giblets from the cavity, then dry the bird with paper towels. Sprinkle 1 tablespoon of the Spice Rub into the cavity of the chicken. Drizzle the bird with the oil and rub the remaining spice all over the chicken.

Hold the bird upright, with the opening of the cavity at the bottom, and lower it onto the can, so the can fits into the cavity. Pull the legs of the chicken forward so the bird stands upright, like it's sitting on a tripod (the can and the two chicken legs make a three-legged tri-pod).

Preheat the grill to high. Carefully carry the chicken on the can to the grill and stand the chicken up in the center of the hot grates. Close the grill and reduce the heat to medium. Cook the chicken until the skin is dark brown and the meat is cooked through (the chicken should register 175°F on a meat thermometer inserted in the thickest part of a thigh, but not touching the bone), about 1 hour. If the chicken starts to brown too quickly, loosely tent the bird with aluminum foil.

When cooked through, remove the chicken, still on the can, from the grill and let it rest for 10 minutes. To serve, carefully lift the chicken off the can, being cautious as it will still be hot. Cut the chicken into pieces and serve with your favorite BBQ Sauce, for dipping.

PIZZA ON THE GRILL Makes 8 Pizzas

The perfect fun activity to get your guests involved in your Backyard Barbecue. Prepare the pizza dough the day before or purchase prepared pizza dough from your local Pizzeria, Italian market or restaurant. Have each guest stretch the dough, (don't worry about perfect round pizzas—these are supposed to be rustic!), throw the dough onto the grill, top it with sauce, cheese and toppings and enjoy!

16 ounces (1 pound) pizza dough

Flour, for rolling out the dough

Extra-virgin olive oil

2 cups prepared tomato sauce

2 cups shredded mozzarella cheese

2 cups shredded Fontina cheese

Pizza Toppings: **Grilled and raw vegetables, proscuitto strips, sausage, pepperoni, pesto, pineapple, basil leaves, fresh mozzarella cheese, crumbled goat cheese, grated Parmesan cheese, red pepper flakes**

Fire up your outdoor grill or stove-top grill to medium-high. In a mixing bowl combine the shredded mozzarella and Fontina.

Cut the pizza dough into 8 equal pieces and press each ball of dough flat on a floured work surface. By hand, stretch each ball of dough into a 5-inch round, as thin as possible. Layer the floured pizza crusts on a cookie sheet in between layers of parchment paper until ready to use.

Lightly brush both sides of the pizza dough rounds with olive oil. Grill the crusts over medium heat until the first side is golden and crisp, about 3 minutes. Turn the crusts over on the grill and spoon about 1/4 cup of tomato sauce onto each pizza. Top with a layer of cheese and your toppings of choice. Cook the pizzas until the cheese is melted and bubbling.

CHEF'S TIP:

Fontina is one of my favorite flavorful melting cheeses. Try using it in your next lasagna, baked pasta dish or melted on a sandwich…Delicious!

BUTTERFLIED LEG OF LAMB PROVENCAL Serves 8

Carve the lamb against the grain and cut it into thin slices, then pile it onto crusty rolls with watercress, mint sauce and grilled fennel. Lamb and rosemary are a match made in heaven....The meat should be tender and flavorful,
with a wonderfully caramelized exterior...and leftovers make great sandwiches!

2 tablespoons fresh thyme leaves, coarsely chopped

2 tablespoons fresh rosemary leaves, coarsely chopped

4 garlic cloves, minced

1/4 cup extra-virgin olive oil

Juice and zest of 2 lemons

Salt & freshly ground pepper

1 (5 pound) Leg of Lamb, trimmed and boned

In a large heavy-duty sealable plastic bag, combine the thyme, rosemary, garlic, olive oil, lemon zest and lemon juice. Place the lamb in the bag, seal and shake to coat. Marinate the lamb in the refrigerator for at least three hours or up to overnight.

Remove the lamb from the refrigerator 30 minutes before ready to grill. Heat your outdoor barbecue to medium heat. Season the lamb with salt and pepper and grill for 25 to 30 minutes for medium rare, turning once during cooking. For medium-rare, a meat thermometer should read 125°F internally. After the lamb rests, the internal temperature will rise to 135°F.

Let the lamb rest for 10 minutes before slicing and serving.

CHEF'S TIP:
You can also roast the Butterflied Leg of Lamb at 375°F for 20 to 25 minutes, then broil on high heat for 3 to 5 minutes more for a caramelized exterior.

WINE TIP:
This flavorful and robust roast stands up to big bold wines, and a perfect pairing will brings out the succulence and meaty flavor of the lamb. Try a Shiraz, Cabernet or my personal pick, a jammy Zinfandel.

SIMPLE & SENSATIONAL
STRAWBERRY CREAM PIE Serves 8

This perfect summer dessert has a crunchy crust and a creamy filling. Let the pie stand at room temperature for ten to fifteen minutes before slicing and serving.

2 cups Nilla wafers

1/4 cup granulated sugar

1 stick (4 ounces) unsalted butter, melted

1 (14 ounce) can sweetened condensed milk

1/4 cup fresh lime juice

1/4 cup fresh orange juice

2 pints fresh strawberries, hulled and sliced

1 cup heavy whipping cream, whipped to stiff peaks

Preheat the oven to 350°F. Combine the cookies and sugar in a food processor and process until fine crumbs form. Add the melted butter and pulse to combine. Press the mixture onto the bottom of an ungreased 10" springform pan. Bake for 10 minutes then allow the crust to cool completely before filling.

Using an electric mixer combine the sweetened condensed, lime juice and orange juice and beat until smooth. Add the sliced strawberries and mix until just combined. By hand, fold the whipped cream into the mixture, then pour into the cooled crust. Cover the pie and freeze until firm, at least 4 hours or overnight.

FIRE UP YOUR BACKYARD BARBEQUE

BLT TOMATO SALAD

~~~~~

ASIAN BEEF SKEWERS

~~~~~

MAPLE BOURBON GLAZED GRILLED CHICKEN

~~~~~

GRILLED SAUSAGE & PEPPER SANDWICHES

~~~~~

SUMMER PASTA SALAD with PECANS and ORANGES

~~~~~

GRILLED ANGEL FOOD CAKE with FRUIT SALSA

BLT TOMATO SALAD Serves 6 to 8

Delicious, quick to prepare easy and flavorful, and a great way to use up summer's sweet tomato crop! For a light weeknight meal, top the salad with grilled chicken or shrimp and a sprinkling of crumbled feta cheese, goat cheese or grated Parmesan.

1 small loaf crusty French or sourdough bread,
   cut into 1-inch cubes

3 cups baby arugula leaves

4 large or 8 small tomatoes, cut into bite-sized pieces

1 large cucumber, seeded and sliced

1 small red onion, diced

1/2 cup pitted Kalamata olives

1/4 cup basil leaves, cut into thin strips

1/4 cup chopped fresh parsley

1 large garlic clove, minced

1 tablespoon fresh lemon juice

1/4 cup red wine vinegar

1/2 cup extra-virgin olive oil

Salt & pepper

8 strips applewood-smoked bacon,
   cooked until crisp and crumbled

In a large salad bowl combine all of the ingredients, except for the bacon. Toss well.

Cover and refrigerate for 30 minutes or up to 3 hours to blend flavors.

Bring to room temperature before serving. Garnish the salad with the crumbled bacon and serve.

ASIAN BEEF SKEWERS Serves 8 as an Appetizer or 4 as a Main Course

These ginger-flavored beef skewers are excellent as an appetizer or terrific on a barbecue buffet. Strips of flank steak are marinated overnight in an exceptionally flavorful marinade and threaded on wooden skewers. Be sure to grill the skewers over a hot flame, to get the beef nice and crusty on both sides and remember to soak the wooden skewers in water for at least 30 minutes before using, so that they don't burn on the grill.

1/4 cup hoisin sauce

1/4 cup dry Sherry

1/4 cup soy sauce

1 tablespoon sesame oil

3 garlic cloves, finely chopped

2 tablespoons finely grated fresh ginger

6 green onions, finely chopped

2 pounds flank steak

In a mixing bowl whisk together the hoisin sauce, sherry, soy sauce, sesame oil, garlic, ginger and half of the green onions.

Slice the flank steak across the grain to make thin slices. Place the flank steak slices in a large sealable plastic bag and pour in the marinade. Refrigerate for at least 2 hours or overnight.

Preheat the grill to high. Drain the steak from the marinade and reserve the marinade. Thread the steak slices on skewers and grill for 2 to 3 minutes or until cooked to the desired doneness.

In a small saucepot, bring the marinade to a full boil, then reduce the heat to low and simmer 5 minutes. Garnish the grilled steak skewers with the remaining freshly chopped green onions and serve with the sauce, for dipping.

MAPLE BOURBON GLAZED GRILLED CHICKEN Serves 6

An easy recipe that will impress your family and friends! Simple grilled chicken gets a burst of fabulous flavor from the bourbon (which also acts as a tenderizer) and the maple syrup caramelizes and sweetens the chicken. Double the glaze and save the leftover sauce for another grilling use; It will keep, covered and chilled for two weeks.

For the Marinade:
1/2 cup freshly squeezed orange juice

1/4 cup freshly squeezed lemon juice

1/4 cup freshly squeezed lime juice

1 teaspoon ground cumin

For the Glaze:
1/3 cup fresh orange juice

1/3 cup pure maple syrup

2 tablespoons Bourbon

2 tablespoons firmly packed brown sugar

1 tablespoon Dijon mustard

1 whole chicken (4 to 5 pounds), cut into pieces

Salt & freshly ground pepper

Combine the orange, lemon and lime juices with the cumin in a large sealable plastic bag. Add the chicken pieces and toss to coat. Marinate the chicken for at least an hour in the refrigerator.

Combine the Glaze ingredients in a small saucepan over medium heat. Bring the mixture to a boil, reduce to a simmer and cook for 5 minutes. Let cool before using.

Preheat the barbecue or a stove-top grill to medium. Remove the chicken from the marinade, pat dry and season with salt and pepper. Place the chicken on the grill and cook for 8 to 10 minutes on the first side. Turn the chicken pieces over and cook for an additional 8 to 10 minutes. After 20 minutes of cooking, begin brushing the chicken with the prepared glaze. Continue to grill the chicken, turning often and brushing with additional glaze, until the chicken is cooked through, about 30 minutes for the breasts and 35 minutes for the thighs and legs.

Remove the chicken from the grill and let stand for 5 minutes before serving. Serve with additional glaze for dipping.

GRILLED SAUSAGE & PEPPER SANDWICHES Serves 8

The smoky flavor from the grill makes these sandwiches taste especially good. We're not green pepper fans, so we use red and yellow bell peppers to add sweetness and color to the dish. This recipe can easily be prepared indoors by sautéing the onions and peppers, along with the sausages, on top of the stove. Be sure to toast the rolls before filling them for a delicious crispy texture.

1/4 cup extra-virgin olive oil	3 yellow bell peppers, thinly sliced
6 red onions, sliced thinly	3 pounds hot or mild Italian sausage
2 garlic cloves, minced	12 fresh basil leaves
1/2 teaspoon dried red chili flakes, or to taste	1 cup dark beer
	1 cup tomato sauce
1/2 teaspoon dried oregano	Salt & freshly ground pepper
3 red bell peppers, thinly sliced	8 Hoagie Rolls

Preheat the barbecue to high. Heat the oil in a large, shallow pot on top of the grill over high heat. Add the onions, season with salt and pepper, and sauté over medium-low heat until tender and caramelized, about 30 minutes. Add the garlic, red chili flakes, oregano and red and yellow bell peppers. Continue sautéing until the peppers are tender.

While the onion/pepper mixture is cooking, grill the sausages until cooked through.

Add the cooked sausages to the cooked onions/peppers along with the basil and the beer. Bring the mixture to a boil, then reduce the heat and simmer until the liquid is almost evaporated. Add the tomato sauce and red pepper flakes and cook 10 minutes longer to combine the flavors.

Serve the sausage & pepper mixture in toasted rolls.

WINE TIP:

Accompany these spicy grilled sausages, with their tomato base, with a lighter red wine like a Sangiovese, Syrah or Merlot. For spicy foods that aren't tomato based, try an off-dry or slightly sweet white wine such as a Riesling.

SUMMER PASTA SALAD
with PECANS and ORANGES Serves 8

This vegetarian dish is ideal as a main course, served with a salad, or as a side dish at a barbecue. Add grilled chicken or shrimp for a light summer meal. The trick to a delicious pasta salad is in adding the dressing to the noodles while they are still warm, so that they absorb the flavors.

1 1/2 cups plain yogurt

1 1/2 cups mayonnaise

2/3 cup freshly squeezed orange juice

1 tablespoon soy sauce

1 tablespoon freshly grated orange zest

2 pounds dried fettuccini

1 1/2 cups pecan halves, coarsely chopped

2 cups mandarin orange segments, drained

2 cups baby arugula leaves

Salt & freshly ground pepper

In a large mixing bowl, whisk together the yogurt, mayonnaise, orange juice, soy sauce and orange zest. Cover and refrigerate until needed.

Preheat the oven to 350°F. Spread the chopped pecans on a baking sheet and bake for about 10 minutes, tossing once, or until toasted and golden.

Cook the fettuccini in boiling salted water according to the package directions. Drain the pasta well and place it in a large mixing bowl.

Add the dressing, toasted pecans, mandarin oranges and arugula to the warm pasta and toss to coat. Season to taste with salt and pepper. Serve warm or cold.

GRILLED ANGEL FOOD CAKE
with FRUIT SALSA   Serves 8

Grilling angel food cake or pound cake intensifies the flavor, and caramelizes the sugar to create toasty sweetness. Be sure to watch the angel food cake very carefully when grilling....Don't walk away from the grill, as it browns very quickly!

For the Fruit Salsa:

1/2 cup papaya or melon,
   seeds removed and diced

1/2 cup fresh strawberries,
   hulled and diced

1/2 cup fresh blueberries

1/2 cup fresh raspberries

3 tablespoons granulated sugar

Juice of half a lime

1/4 cup fresh mint leaves, cut into thin strips

For the Raspberry Sauce:

2 cups fresh raspberries

1/4 cup Chambord or Grand Marnier

3 tablespoons granulated sugar,
   or more to taste

Juice of half a lemon

1 (14 ounce) angel food cake

To make the Fruit Salsa, in a mixing bowl, combine the fruit, sugar, lime juice and mint and mix well. Set aside.

To make the Raspberry Sauce, puree all of the ingredients in a food processor or blender. Strain the sauce to remove the seeds. Store in the refrigerator until ready to use.

Preheat the barbecue or a stove-top grill to high. Slice the cake in half horizontally and place both sides, cut side down, on the grill. Grill for 30 to 60 seconds or until golden brown and toasted, then turn the cake halves over and grill the other sides until golden. Place one half of the cake on a plate or cake stand and drizzle with Raspberry Sauce. Place the other half of the cake on top and fill the center of the cake with the fruit salsa.

Cut slices and serve, garnished with additional Raspberry Sauce.

A Family Picnic Outing

FENNEL AND APPLE SLAW

CRISPY DIJON CHICKEN

LEMON BASIL POTATO SALAD

CHOCOLATE ESPRESSO COOKIES

FENNEL and APPLE SLAW Serves 6

This light and refreshing slaw is best eaten the same day. Slice the fennel on a mandolin, if you have one, or use a sharp knife to shave the fennel as thinly as possible.

1/4 cup golden raisins

Juice of 1 orange

1 tablespoon balsamic vinegar

2 fennel bulbs, trimmed and thinly sliced

2 green apples – cored, quartered and thinly sliced

1 bunch watercress, stems removed and coarsely chopped

3 tablespoons chopped fresh chives

2 tablespoons chopped fresh parsley

1/2 cup sliced almonds, toasted

3 to 4 tablespoons extra-virgin olive oil

Salt & freshly ground pepper

Combine the raisins, orange juice and balsamic vinegar in a small saucepot. Bring the mixture to a simmer over medium heat, then remove from the heat and let sit 10 minutes to plump the raisins.

Combine the fennel, apple slices, watercress, chives and parsley in a large mixing bowl. Add the plumped raisins along with the plumping liquid. Add the almonds and drizzle the slaw with the olive oil to lightly coat. Toss well. Season with salt and pepper to taste. Refrigerate until ready to serve.

CRISPY DIJON CHICKEN Serves 6

This chicken dish is highlighted by the pungent flavors of the mustard marinade and is perfect served hot or cold. The Panko crumbs, with their flaky texture, impart a delicious crunch. Try slicing the crispy chicken over a salad or serve the chicken with some quickly stir-fried vegetables for a simpler dinner.

4 tablespoons plus 2 tablespoons extra-virgin olive oil

1/3 cup Dijon mustard

3 garlic cloves, minced

Juice of 2 lemons

1 tablespoon soy sauce

Salt & freshly ground pepper

6 boneless, skinless chicken breasts or chicken thighs

2 cups Panko (Japanese bread crumbs) or seasoned bread crumbs

In a mixing bowl whisk together the 4 tablespoons of olive oil, Dijon mustard, garlic, lemon juice and soy sauce. Place the chicken pieces in a sealable plastic bag and pour in the marinade. Marinate the chicken for at least 4 hours, preferably overnight.

When ready to cook, preheat the oven to 375°F. In the bag, season the chicken with salt and pepper, then remove the chicken pieces from them marinade and immediately coat the wet chicken with the bread crumbs, shaking off any excess.

Heat the remaining 2 tablespoons of olive oil in a large oven-proof sauté pan until hot. Add the breaded chicken to the pan and sauté until golden on one side. Turn the chicken breasts over and immediately place the pan in the oven to finish cooking. Bake the chicken for 10 to 15 minutes, depending on the thickness of the breasts, and the thighs for 20 to 25 minutes, or until the chicken is cooked through.

WINE TIP:
Try the rich flavor of a Viognier or Chardonnay with this dish.
Both Chardonnay and Viognier share tropical fruit flavors and a
creamy mouthfeel.

LEMON BASIL POTATO SALAD Serves 8

The perfect summer side dish....safe to take to a picnic or to put on an outdoor buffet. Adding the dressing to the warm potatoes allows the flavors to soak in wonderfully. Serve the potato salad at room temperature.

2 pounds small Yukon Gold potatoes or new potatoes,
   cut into quarters

Extra-virgin olive oil

12 peeled garlic cloves, left whole

Salt & freshly ground pepper

1/4 cup fresh lemon juice

3/4 cup loosely packed fresh basil

1 tablespoon Dijon mustard

Salt & freshly ground pepper to taste

2/3 cup extra-virgin olive oil

2 cups fresh baby spinach leaves

Preheat the oven to 400°F. In a large mixing bowl toss the potatoes and garlic cloves with a drizzle of olive oil to lightly coat. Season with salt and pepper. Arrange the potatoes and garlic cloves in a single layer on a baking sheet and roast for 30 to 35 minutes, tossing occasionally, until tender and golden.

Using a blender or food processor, combine the lemon juice, basil and Dijon mustard. Slowly pour in the oil in a slow, steady stream, with the blender running, to create an emulsified dressing. Season the dressing to taste with salt and pepper.

Place the warm roasted potatoes, roasted garlic cloves, spinach leaves, and cherry tomatoes in a large mixing bowl. Toss with the dressing to coat well.

CHEF'S TIP:

I love making salad dressings and marinades in the blender because you're guaranteed a blended success and because it eliminates all the whisking. Adding a teaspoon of Dijon mustard to your dressing will help the oil blend with the acid to make an emulsified dressing.

CHOCOLATE ESPRESSO COOKIES Makes 36 Cookies

What could be better than deep, dense chocolate and dark espresso combined in a rich cookie?

1 stick (4 ounces) unsalted butter

4 ounces unsweetened chocolate

1/4 cup chocolate-covered espresso beans, coarsely chopped

4 large eggs

2 cups granulated sugar

2 teaspoons pure vanilla extract

1 1/2 cups all-purpose flour

1/2 cup unsweetened cocoa powder

2 teaspoons baking powder

Pinch of salt

In a double boiler, melt the butter with the chocolate until smooth. Or, melt the butter with the chocolate in the microwave on 50% power, in 30-second increments. Add the chopped espresso beans and cool the mixture to room temperature.

Using an electric mixer, beat the eggs, sugar, and vanilla until thick and lemon colored, about five minutes. Mix in the chocolate mixture. Combine the flour, cocoa, baking powder and salt in a mixing bowl and add the dry mixture to the egg mixture. Mix just until incorporated. Do not overmix. Chill the dough for one hour before proceeding.

Preheat the oven to 350°F. Line cookie sheets with silicone baking mats or parchment paper. Using wet hands, spoon golf ball-sized scoops of the cookie dough and roll to form round balls. Place the balls 2-inches apart on the prepared cookie sheet. Bake for 10 to 12 minutes, or until the cookies are firm on the edges, but still soft in the center. Cool the cookies on the sheet for five minutes, then remove to a rack to finish cooling. Store the cookies in an airtight container.

Kids In The Kitchen!

OLD-FASHIONED COUNTRY FAIR LEMONADE

~~~~~~

HOMEMADE CORNDOGS

~~~~~~

POPCORN BALLS

~~~~~~

PEANUT BUTTER CUPCAKES

OLD-FASHIONED COUNTRY FAIR LEMONADE

An old-fashioned summertime treat...Thirst quenching and not too sweet!
Prepare the lemon syrup in advance, so that you can easily make lemonade
any time.

> **2 cups granulated sugar**
>
> **2 cups water**
>
> **Juice of 8 lemons**
>
> **2 lemons, sliced into rings**

In a medium saucepan, combine the sugar and water. Bring the mixture to a boil,
then simmer over medium heat for 5 minutes to make a simple syrup. Let the
syrup cool completely before proceeding.

Add the lemon juice and lemon slices to the syrup. Cover and let stand 1 hour.
Strain the lemon syrup into a jar or pitcher. Store in the refrigerator until ready to use.

For each serving, put 1/3 cup lemon syrup into an 8 ounce glass; fill with ice
cubes and cold water. Stir and serve.

HOMEMADE CORNDOGS Makes 8 Corn Dogs

In the early 1940s, a delicious deep-fried version of the hot dog debuted at the Texas State Fair. It's still a favorite of kids and adults alike! Spice up your corndogs by adding hot peppers, onions, or shredded cheese to the batter.

1 cup yellow cornmeal

1 cup all-purpose flour

2 teaspoons salt

1 teaspoon baking powder

A pinch of baking soda

1 1/2 cups buttermilk

8 hot dogs

8 wooden skewers

Canola Oil

Heat the oil in a deep fryer or large stockpot to 375°F.

Whisk together all of the ingredients but do not over stir the batter; it should be a little lumpy. Dry the hot dogs with paper towels to remove any moisture and to insure that the batter sticks. Place the hot dogs on the wooden skewers, then dip the dogs into the batter.

Gently place the battered hot dogs into the oil, leaving the exposed part of the stick outside of the oil. Fry the corndogs until golden.

POPCORN BALLS

Sweet, salty and delicious. Moms and Dads, please be cautious when kids are forming the popcorns balls as the mixture is hot. For Chocoholics, add mini chocolate chips, for Peanut Lovers add roasted peanuts...If you like sweet and spicy flavors, try adding Red Hots....Oh, the possibilities are endless!

6 tablespoons unsalted butter

1 10-ounce bag mini marshmallows

1/4 cup brown sugar

8 cups popped salted popcorn

Unsalted butter

Melt the butter in a large heavy stockpot. Add the marshmallows and the sugar and stir until melted. Remove from the heat and stir in the popcorn. Butter your hands and shape the balls into desired sizes. Set on a parchment paper or silicone-lined cookie sheet to set.

For PEANUT BUTTER POPCORN BALLS, reduce the butter to 4 tablespoons and add 1/3 cup creamy Peanut Butter.

To color the popcorn balls, add a few drops of food coloring to the smooth marshmallow mixture. Mix well to distribute the color evenly, then continue with the recipe as instructed above.

PEANUT BUTTER CUPCAKES Makes 12 Cupcakes

For kids of all ages, we love cupcakes because they come in cute individual packages. Variations abound on this come-back dessert...You can serve them warm from the oven without frosting, or dip the tops of the cupcakes in melted chocolate for a stupendous treat.

1 stick plus 2 tablespoons unsalted butter, at room temperature

1 cup creamy peanut butter

3/4 cup granulated sugar

3 large eggs

1 3/4 cups all-purpose flour

2 teaspoons baking powder

Preheat the oven to 325°F. Using an electric mixer beat the butter, peanut butter and sugar until light and fluffy. Add the eggs, flour and baking powder and beat until well combined.

Spoon the mixture into a paper-lined cupcake tin, filling the cups three-quarters full. Bake for 20 minutes.

CHEF'S TIP:
Add mini chocolate chips or chopped peanuts to the batter
for extra special cakelets.

A Friend Caught-A-Fish Dinner
(or Trapped a Crab, or Netted a Lobster!)

WHOLE ROASTED SALMON with LEMON and FENNEL

~~~

PROSCIUTTO-WRAPPED HALIBUT with WHITE BEANS

~~~

CHINESE STEAMED FISH

~~~

OVEN-ROASTED CRAB

~~~

LOBSTER SALAD

WHOLE ROASTED SALMON with LEMON and FENNEL Serves 8

After a successful fishing trip, a friend brought us two very large, beautiful salmon, which we roasted with lemon and fennel, thus creating this delicious recipe. Serve the salmon with roasted Yukon gold potatoes and steamed asparagus topped with lemon zest and bread crumbs.

6 tablespoons extra-virgin olive oil

2 fennel bulbs, thinly sliced

4 tablespoons fennel seeds

4 whole lemons – 3 thinly sliced and 1 juiced

6 garlic cloves, minced

2 cups dry white wine

1 whole salmon (about 6 pounds), gutted and scaled

1 bunch fresh Italian parsley

Salt & freshly ground pepper

Garnish: 3 bunches fresh herbs (parsley, thyme, dill)

Preheat the oven to 450°F. Brush a large roasting pan with 2 tablespoons of the olive oil. Place half of the sliced fennel, half of the lemon slices, half of the fennel seeds and half of the chopped garlic on the bottom of the roasting pan to form a bed.

Season the cavity of the salmon with salt and pepper. Place the entire bunch of parsley and one lemon, sliced, inside the cavity. Lay the salmon into the pan and season the surface of the fish with salt and pepper. Spread the remaining fennel, lemon slices, fennel seeds and garlic evenly on top of the fish. Drizzle the lemon juice and olive oil on top of the fish. Pour the white wine into the roasting pan around the salmon.

Place the pan in the oven to roast and baste the salmon with the liquid in the bottom of the pan after 10 minutes of cooking.

After 25 minutes, check for doneness by inserting an instant read thermometer into the salmon, without touching the spine. The internal temperature should read 135°F in the thickest part of the fish.

Place the whole fish on a serving platter, peel off the skin and garnish the platter with fresh bunches of herbs. Scatter the fennel from the roasting pan around the platter and serve.

WINE TIP:

While the rule has always been "White Wine with Fish", it doesn't always make the perfect pairing. A white wine with high alcohol paired with salmon often makes the wine taste too pungent. So, I recommend that you break the rules and try a slightly chilled California Pinot Noir or French Beaujolais with the Roasted Salmon. Try it...It's a delicious match!

PROSCIUTTO-WRAPPED HALIBUT with WHITE BEANS Serves 4

Fabulous foods don't have to be fattening! We love this delicious recipe because it satisfies your palate without expanding your waistline. It uses delicious prosciutto, my favorite aged, cured Italian ham, which when combined with a mild fish such as halibut, adds flavor, moisture and crunch. Pair the dish with a Viognier for the perfect compliment.

4 (6 ounce) skinless halibut fillets

8 paper-thin slices prosciutto

3 tablespoons extra-virgin olive oil

2 cups canned or jarred cooked large white beans, drained

1 cup cherry tomatoes, halved

2 tablespoons balsamic vinegar

1/4 cup chopped fresh parsley

Salt & freshly ground pepper

Garnish: 1 lemon, cut into 6 wedges

Preheat the oven to 350°F. Wrap each halibut fillet with 2 slices of prosciutto, leaving 1/2-inch of the fish exposed at each end.

Heat one tablespoon of olive oil in a large, heavy non-stick sauté pan over high heat. Add the wrapped fish fillets and sear on one side until the prosciutto is crispy, about 2 minutes. Turn the fillets over and place the pan in the oven to cook the fish all the way through, about 5 minutes.

In a separate sauté pan heat the remaining two tablespoons of olive oil over medium heat. Add the beans, tomatoes and balsamic vinegar and sauté until beans are heated through and vinegar has reduced, about 3 minutes. Add the chopped parsley and season with salt and pepper, to taste.

To serve, spoon the bean mixture onto each plate, top with a halibut fillet and serve with a wedge of lemon.

CHINESE STEAMED FISH Serves 4

Halibut, cod or any firm-fleshed white fish will work in this recipe. This is one of those recipes that's easy to prepare, incredibly moist and flavorful and hard to mess up. Serve over white rice with the sauce spooned over or with stir-fried snow peas, broccoli and water chestnuts.

> **2 ounces dried porcini mushrooms**
>
> **1 cup boiling water**
>
> **1 pound whitefish fillets**
>
> **1 tablespoon soy sauce**
>
> **1 tablespoon freshly grated ginger root**
>
> **2 green onions, thinly sliced**
>
> <u>**Garnish:**</u> **1 teaspoon sesame oil**
>
>   **2 green onions, thinly sliced**

Place the dried mushrooms in a small mixing bowl and pour the boiling water over the mushrooms. Let the mushrooms soak for 15 minutes, then drain, reserving the liquid. Slice the mushrooms into thin strips.

In a sauteuse (a straight-sided sauté pan), combine the sliced mushrooms, reserved mushroom soaking liquid, soy sauce, ginger and green onions. Place the fish fillets into the liquid. Place the pan over medium heat on top of the stove and bring the liquid to a simmer. Once gently simmering, lower the heat and cover the pan. Steam the fillets until cooked through, about 7 to 10 minutes for 1-inch thick fillets.

To serve, remove the fish from the liquid and drizzle with the sesame oil. Garnish with the chopped green onions.

OVEN-ROASTED CRAB Serves 4

I love this recipe! Spicy and delicious, this dish serves as a casual weekday meal or a perfect Saturday night dinner that guarantees to garner compliments. Serve crusty Sourdough bread alongside to soak up the butter and an organic green salad with a simple vinaigrette. Crab pairs perfectly with a bright, crisp Sauvignon Blanc or a buttery Chardonnay.

4 tablespoons unsalted butter

1/4 cup extra-virgin olive oil

3 garlic cloves, minced

2 tablespoons minced shallot

1 teaspoon dried red pepper flakes

1 teaspoon garlic powder

3 large Dungeness crabs (about 5 pounds) – cooked, cleaned and cracked

3 tablespoons chopped fresh parsley

1/2 cup dry white wine

Zest of 1 orange

Zest of 1 lemon

1/4 cup fresh orange juice

1/4 cup fresh lemon juice

<u>Garnish:</u> 1/4 cup chopped green onions

Preheat the oven to 500°F.

Melt the butter with the oil in a large ovenproof skillet over high heat. Stir in the garlic, shallot, red pepper flakes and the garlic powder. Add the crabs and the parsley and stir to combine. Place the skillet in the oven and roast the crabs until heated through, stirring once, about 15 minutes.

Using tongs, transfer the crabs to a platter. Place the pan over medium heat and add the wine, orange zest, lemon zest, orange and lemon juice. Boil the sauce until it is reduced by about half, about 5 minutes. Add the crabs back to the skillet and toss to coat well. Garnish with the green onions and serve family style.

CHEF'S TIP:
Did you know that most supermarkets will steam crabs, boil lobsters and sometimes even marinate fish fillets for you? Ask the fish monger to steam the crabs and crack them for you to make this recipe truly simple.

LOBSTER SALAD Serves 4

This salad is best eaten a few hours after it is made, but it will keep in the refrigerator for 2 days. Its beautiful colors and rich taste are perfect for a family-style buffet or to use in sandwiches.

2 cups cooked lobster meat (2 1/2-pound to 3-pound lobster)

1/2 fennel bulb, trimmed and diced

2 celery stalks, diced

3 tablespoons yellow onion, minced

1 small garlic clove, minced

1/2 shallot, minced

1 tablespoon chopped fresh parsley

1 tablespoon chopped fresh chives

1 lemon, zested and juiced

1/4 cup mayonnaise

1 tablespoon crème fraiche or sour cream

Salt & freshly ground pepper

Combine all of the ingredients in a mixing bowl and season to taste with salt and pepper. Refrigerate the lobster salad for at least half an hour before serving.

Serve in toasted rolls or on top of greens.

HOMEMADE CREME FRAICHE Makes 1 1/2 cups

Crème Fraiche is a thickened cream with a slightly tangy flavor and an incredibly rich texture. It is the ideal addition to sauces or soups because it can be boiled without curdling and it makes a delicious accompaniment to fresh fruit or on top of desserts, in place of whipped cream. (You can buy it in the cheese section in most markets, if you choose not to make it.)

1 cup heavy cream

1/2 cup sour cream

Whisk together the heavy cream and sour cream and pour the mixture into a Mason jar. Refrigerate for 12 hours, or until thick. Store in the refrigerator for up to 2 weeks.

Autumn Nights

CAULIFLOWER SOUP with GORGONZOLA CHEESE

~~~~~

CJ'S GOOD, SIMPLE SALAD

~~~~~

HEARTY BEEF STEW IN RED WINE

~~~~~

SAFFRON NOODLES

~~~~~

HOMEMADE CHICKEN POT PIE

~~~~~

DOUBLE DIPPED APRICOTS

CAULIFLOWER SOUP
with GORGONZOLA CHEESE Serves 6

This is a simple yet rich soup, made scrumptious with crumbled gorgonzola cheese. Use an immersion blender, if you have one, to puree the soup in the pot and serve the soup with a rustic salad and crusty bread, for the perfect cold-weather meal. Use any good-quality blue-veined cheese you like.

3 tablespoons unsalted butter

1 small yellow onion, diced

1 garlic clove, minced

1 small head cauliflower, cored and cut into equal-sized florets

2 1/2 cups whole milk

1/2 cup heavy whipping cream

Pinch of freshly grated nutmeg

Salt & freshly ground pepper

Garnish: 1 cup crumbled Gorgonzola cheese

Melt the butter in a soup pot over medium heat. Add the onion and sauté until tender and translucent, about 10 minutes. Add the garlic and sauté one minute more. Add the cauliflower, milk and cream and bring the soup to a simmer. Do not boil. Simmer the soup for 20 minutes or until the cauliflower is very tender.

Using a blender, puree the soup in batches until smooth. Return the soup to the pot and season with nutmeg, salt and pepper.

Serve the soup in warm bowls topped with crumbled Gorgonzola cheese.

CJ'S GOOD, SIMPLE SALAD Serves 4

This is one of my favorite salads. Depending on the season, I like to substitute dried cranberries, cherries or apricots for the strawberries.

1 head Bibb lettuce, washed and torn into pieces

3 cups (1 bag) baby arugula leaves

1 red onion, thinly sliced

1 pint strawberries, thinly sliced

1 cup walnut pieces, toasted

For the Dressing:

1 teaspoon Dijon mustard

1/4 cup raspberry vinegar

1/4 cup walnut oil

1/2 cup grapeseed oil

Salt & freshly ground pepper

Garnish: Crumbled goat cheese

Toss the Bibb lettuce, arugula, onion, strawberries and walnuts in a large salad bowl.

Using a blender or whisking by hand, combine the Dijon mustard and vinegar. With the blender running, slowly pour in the walnut oil and grapeseed oil in a slow, steady stream to create an emulsified dressing. Season the dressing to taste with salt and pepper.

Toss with the salad with the dressing just before serving. Serve on chilled plates and garnish each plate with crumbled goat cheese.

CHEF'S TIP:

Grapeseed Oil, with its extremely high smoking point, is also terrific for sautéing and high-heat cooking, and it has no flavor transference... It's totally neutral.

HEARTY BEEF STEW IN RED WINE Serves 6

This hearty beef stew is heart-warming comfort food and tastes fabulous served over Saffron Noodles. It benefits from being prepared in advance and reheated, and leftovers freeze very well.

1 bottle dry red wine	1 sprig fresh thyme
6 tablespoons olive oil	1 bay leaf
All-purpose flour, for dredging	6 black peppercorns
3 pounds lean boneless chuck roast, cut in 1 1/2 inch cubes	Salt and freshly ground black pepper
2 large yellow onions	6 carrots, peeled and cut into large chunks
4 garlic cloves, minced	1/4 pound fresh mushroom caps
4 tablespoons Cognac	1 (8 ounce) bag frozen petite peas
3 cups beef broth	
	Garnish: Freshly chopped parsley

Pour the bottle of wine into a small saucepan and bring to a simmer over medium heat. Simmer the wine until reduced by half.

Heat three tablespoons of the olive oil in a large pot over high heat. Place the flour in a large shallow bowl and season the flour generously with salt and pepper. Dredge the cubes of beef in the flour, shaking off any excess. In batches, add enough floured beef to the pan to fill the pan in a single layer, and sauté until the meat is caramelized on all sides. Remove the meat with a slotted spoon and set aside. Add two more tablespoons of oil to the pan and repeat with the remaining beef. Remove the beef and set aside.

continued

HEARTY BEEF STEW IN RED WINE continued

Add one tablespoon of oil to the same pot along with the diced onion. Sauté until tender, about 10 minutes. Add the garlic and cook 2 minutes more. Add the Cognac to the pan and scrape up any caramelized bits from the bottom of the pan. Add the reduced wine, beef broth, thyme, bay leaf, sugar and peppercorns to the pot along with the browned meat. Bring the mixture to a boil, reduce the heat to a simmer, cover the pot and cook over low heat for 2 hours.

After 2 hours, add the carrots and mushrooms to the pot. Simmer the stew for 30 minutes more, until the vegetables and meat are tender. Add the frozen peas during the last two minutes of cooking. Adjust the seasoning and serve over Saffron Noodles. Garnish with parsley.

SAFFRON NOODLES Serves 6 to 8

1/2 pound dried fettuccine

1/2 teaspoon crushed saffron threads

Salt

2 tablespoons unsalted butter

Bring a large pot of water to a boil. Add a large tablespoon of salt and the saffron threads to the boiling water. Bring the water back to a boil, then drop in the pasta. As soon as the noodles soften into the pot, stir to keep the noodles from sticking together. (Do NOT add oil to the water as the saffron will not infuse into the noodles!)

Cook to the desired doneness, then drain the pasta well and toss with the butter before serving.

CHEF'S TIP:

Saffron is the most expensive spice in the world. Available in threads and ground, I recommend you cook with the threads. Not only will they retain their flavor longer, but you are assured you have purchased pure saffron. Powdered saffron tends to have less pungency and is often mixed with fillers.

HOMEMADE CHICKEN POT PIE Serves 8

This Pot Pie is made easy by using leftover roast chicken or by buying a rotisserie chicken from the deli section at your local supermarket.

1 sheet frozen puff pastry, thawed	2 cups chicken broth
5 tablespoons all-purpose flour,	1 cup whole milk
plus more for dusting	4 cups cooked chicken, cubed
5 tablespoons unsalted butter	1 cup frozen green peas
1 large onion, chopped	2 tablespoons parsley, chopped
2 medium potatoes,	2 tablespoons fresh thyme leaves,
peeled and cut into 1-inch pieces	picked from the stems
4 carrots, peeled and cut into 1-inch pieces	Hot Sauce, to taste
12 ounces sliced mushroom	Salt & freshly ground pepper
1/3 cup brandy	1 egg, beaten

Place the puff pastry on a cutting board and invert a 3-quart round casserole or soufflé dish onto the top of it. With a sharp knife, cut around the casserole, allowing for a 1-inch overhang. Place the puff pastry sheet on a cookie sheet and chill until ready to bake.

In a large pot, melt the butter over medium heat. Add the onion, potatoes and carrots and season with salt and pepper. Sauté, stirring occasionally, until potatoes and carrots are tender, about 10 minutes. Add the mushrooms and cook for 2 minutes. Add the cognac and cook for 30 seconds. Add the flour and cook 1 minute more. Pour in the chicken broth and milk and bring to a simmer. Cook until thick, about 2 minutes. Stir in the chicken, peas, parsley, thyme and hot sauce. Adjust the seasoning. Transfer to the 3-quart casserole or soufflé dish.

Preheat the oven to 400°F. Remove the puff pastry from the refrigerator and brush the surface evenly with the beaten egg. Invert the puff pastry and place the egg washed side directly over the casserole, pressing lightly to seal the overhanging crust to the side of the dish. Brush the top surface of dough with the remaining egg wash and cut a small circle in the center of the pastry, to allow the steam to vent.

Transfer the casserole to a baking sheet and bake for 20 minutes or until the pastry is golden and flaky.

DOUBLE DIPPED APRICOTS Makes about 35 Dipped Apricots

Store this delicious confection in an airtight container for up to 2 days or freeze the dipped apricots for up to 2 months.

8 ounces high-quality bittersweet chocolate, chopped

    (I prefer Valrhona, Scharffenberger or Callebaut)

8 ounces white chocolate

2 tablespoons unsalted butter

1 pound fancy dried apricots

Line a baking sheet with a silicone baking mat or parchment paper.

Combine the bittersweet chocolate and 1 tablespoon of the butter in a microwave-safe bowl and microwave on 50% power, in 30-second increments, until melted.

Dip each apricot halfway into the melted bittersweet chocolate, then place the apricot on the baking sheet. Refrigerate the apricots to set the chocolate.

Meanwhile, combine the white chocolate with the remaining tablespoon of butter in a microwave-safe bowl and microwave on 50% power, in 30-second increments, until melted.

Once the bittersweet chocolate has set, dip the other side of the apricots into the melted white chocolate and refrigerate to set.

It's An Open-House... Soup's On!

HEIRLOOM TOMATO SOUP

~~~~~

WILD MUSHROOM SOUP

~~~~~

CARROT GINGER SOUP

~~~~~

ROASTED BEET SOUP

~~~~~

HERB AND PARMESAN MONKEY BREAD

HEIRLOOM TOMATO SOUP Serves 6 to 8

This no-cook soup is full of flavor from the ripe tomatoes of the season, and the olive oil and balsamic brighten this bowl of summer essence. Use a combination of heirloom tomatoes (our dear friend Gloria grows the best tomatoes!), red, yellow, orange, etc., for the best flavor and color.

4 to 6 large Heirloom tomatoes

2 tablespoons good quality extra-virgin olive oil

1 tablespoons good quality aged balsamic vinegar

2 cloves raw or roasted garlic

4 fresh basil leaves

Salt & white pepper to taste

Garnish: Homemade croutons

    Grilled shrimp

    Crème fraiche or sour cream

    Basil Oil or Truffle Oil

Place all of the ingredients in the blender and blend until smooth. Chill before serving.

Garnish with homemade croutons, grilled shrimp, a dollop of crème fraiche, a drizzle of truffle oil, or....

WILD MUSHROOM SOUP Serves 4

For best appearance, be sure to add the cream to the soup just before serving.

2 ounces dried porcini mushrooms

1 cup boiling water

1/3 cup extra-virgin olive oil

1 pound fresh shiitake mushrooms

1 pound fresh cremini (brown) mushrooms, stemmed
   and sliced

1/2 cup shallots, minced

1/2 cup dry white wine

3 cups chicken broth

2 teaspoons fresh thyme leaves, chopped

1/4 cup heavy whipping cream

Salt & freshly ground pepper

To reconstitute the dried mushrooms, cover the dried mushrooms with the boiling water and let soak for 15 minutes, then drain and reserve the soaking liquid. Preheat the oven to 400° F. Place the olive oil in a large roasting pan. Add the fresh and reconstituted mushrooms, salt and pepper and toss well. Roast for 20 minutes, then add the shallots, toss, and continue to roast for 20 minutes more. Remove the roasting pan from the oven, remove 1 cup of the mushrooms and set aside.

Pour the wine into the roasting pan with the remaining mushrooms and scrape the browned bits from the bottom of the pan. Transfer the mixture to a large saucepot and add the chicken broth, the reserved mushroom soaking liquid and the thyme. Cook over medium heat on the top of the stove for 20 minutes.

In a blender, puree the soup in batches. Add the pureed soup back to the pot and add the cream. Bring the soup back to a simmer and adjust the seasoning. Do not boil. Serve in warm bowls, topped with the reserved roasted mushrooms.

CARROT GINGER SOUP Serves 6

You can add butternut squash to this recipe to add a unique quality to the pureed soup. The soup, packed with vitamins A and C, is absolutely lovely ladled into serving bowls, drizzled with a thin swirl of mascarpone cream and topped with frizzled leeks.

2 tablespoons extra-virgin olive oil

1/2 yellow onion, diced

2 tablespoons freshly grated ginger

1 1/2 pounds carrots, peeled and chopped

Pinch of ground nutmeg

1 cup fresh orange juice

4 cups chicken broth or vegetable broth

1/2 cup Half and Half

1 tablespoon unsalted butter, kept cold

Salt & white pepper to taste

Garnish: Fried Leeks

    Mascarpone Cream

Heat the oil in a large saucepan over medium-high heat. Add the onion and sauté until tender, about 10 minutes. Add the ginger, carrots and nutmeg and sauté 2 minutes more. Add the orange juice and chicken broth and simmer the soup until the carrots are tender, about 30 minutes.

Working in batches, puree the mixture in a blender (or use an immersion blender to puree the soup in the pot). Return the soup to the saucepan and stir in the Half and Half. Bring the soup to a simmer (do not boil) and adjust the seasoning.

To make the Mascarpone Cream combine mascarpone cheese with just enough milk or cream to thin the cheese to "drizzling" consistency. Ladle the soup into warm bowls, garnish and serve.

CHEF'S TIP:

To make the frizzled or fried leeks, heat 2 cups of vegetable oil in a medium saucepot to 350°F. Clean the leeks well and cut them into very thin strips, about 2-inches long. Dust the leeks with flour, shaking off any excess, and fry until golden brown, about 30 seconds. Drain on a paper towel and season with salt before using.

ROASTED BEET SOUP Serves 6

This beautiful soup is simple to make and so visually appealing. We like to combine a variety of colored beets; red beets, golden beets or candy cane beets (very mellow beet flavor), for added flavor and color. Serve the soup in warm bowls with a dollop of crème fraiche on top and parmesan breadsticks along side.

> 1 pound beets (about 6 medium beets)
>
> 2 tablespoons unsalted butter
>
> 1 tablespoon extra-virgin olive oil
>
> 1 leek (white and pale green parts only), chopped
>
> 1/8 teaspoon freshly ground nutmeg
>
> 4 cups chicken broth or vegetable broth
>
> 1 bay leaf
>
> 2 fresh thyme sprigs
>
> 1/4 cup heavy whipping cream
>
> Salt & freshly ground pepper
>
> For Garnish: 1/2 cup crème fraîche or sour cream

Preheat the oven to 350°F. Wrap the beets in foil and roast until tender when pierced with a sharp knife, about 1 hour. Cool the beets, then rub each beet between paper towels to remove the skins. Cut the beets into 1-inch pieces.

Melt the butter with the oil in a large pot over medium heat. Add the leeks and cook until tender and golden, stirring often, about 10 minutes. Add the roasted cubed beets and the nutmeg and sauté 10 minutes more. Add the broth, bay leaf and thyme sprigs. Bring the soup to a boil, then reduce the heat to low and simmer for 20 minutes.

Remove the bay leaf and thyme sprigs and discard. Working in batches, puree the soup in a blender. Return the soup to the pot and add the cream. Season to taste with salt and pepper. Bring the soup back to a simmer before serving.

To serve the soup at a later time, cool and refrigerate the soup, then gently rewarm the soup over low heat when ready to serve; Do not boil.

HERB and PARMESAN MONKEY BREAD Serves 8

It's easy to become hooked on this tender pull-apart loaf, hot from the oven. Watch it disappear when served alongside a steaming bowl of soup or with a main course to sop up any sauce left on your plate. Baking bread has never been so easy or so delicious.

> 9 ounces Frozen Bread Dough, thawed
>> (use 1 1/2 loaves of thawed Bridgford Bread Dough
>> or 12 thawed Bridgford Parkerhouse Rolls)
>
> 1 stick (4 ounces) unsalted butter
> 2 garlic cloves, minced
> 2 cups grated Parmesan cheese
> 3 tablespoons chopped fresh rosemary
> 3 tablespoons chopped fresh thyme
> 3 tablespoons chopped fresh parsley
> Freshly ground pepper

Preheat the oven to 350°F. Butter a bundt or tube pan.

Combine the butter and garlic in a microwave-safe shallow bowl and microwave until the butter is completely melted. In another shallow mixing bowl combine the Parmesan cheese with the fresh herbs and pepper.

Cut the thawed dough into 24 equal pieces and gently roll each piece of dough into a ball. Drop a few balls of dough at a time into the melted butter and coat the dough well. Then drop the dough into the cheese mixture and toss to coat. Place the coated pieces into the prepared pan, staggering the balls to create the pull-apart effect after baking. Continue the process with the remaining balls of dough. Let the dough rise until doubled in size.

Bake for 20 minutes then reduce the oven temperature to 325°F and bake for 15 minutes more or until golden brown (the top of the bread should sound hollow when tapped). Remove the monkey bread from the oven and cool slightly before inverting.

CHEF'S TIP:

For a sweet Monkey Bread, eliminate the Parmesan cheese and herb blend and roll the buttered balls of dough in a mixture of 1 cup of granulated sugar combined with 1 cup of finely chopped pecans and 2 teaspoons of ground cinnamon. This deliciously gooey version has great kid appeal!

SOUP AND CONDIMENT BAR

Let your family and friends jazz up these homemade or storebought soups with these condiment ideas:

TOMATO SOUP

Fried tortilla shards, small pasta shapes, vegetable salsas, diced onions, jalapeno rings, pepperoni slices, julienned ham, sour cream, olives, cooked baby shrimp

CHICKEN SOUP

Assorted noodles, mini matzo balls, fried or grilled chunks of chicken, blanched veggies such as peas, carrots or celery, ratatouille, boiled diced potato, rice, chopped hard-boiled egg, toasted raviolis

CHEESE SOUP

Bacon bits, grated cheese, blanched broccoli, mixed chopped herbs, spicy tomato salsa, garlic croutons, asparagus pieces, roasted peppers

WE'RE HAVING A PASTA PARTY!

THE ULTIMATE 5-CHEESE MACARONI & CHEESE

~~~~~~

OUR TWO FAVORITE RISOTTOS

~~~~~~

LITTLE EARS WITH TOMATOES AND TWO CHEESES

~~~~~~

15-MINUTE LASAGNA

THE ULTIMATE 5-CHEESE MACARONI & CHEESE Serves 6

A true family favorite, this recipe is prepared on the stovetop and finished in the oven and it's the richest and most delicious Mac & Cheese you might ever taste. While you set the table, toss a salad of greens with sliced pear, candied walnuts and dried cranberries and open a bottle of Zinfandel. The aroma of bubbling, golden cheese will bring everyone to the table smiling!

1 pound small pasta shells

For the Topping:
1/2 cup Japanese bread crumbs (Panko)
1 cup grated Parmesan cheese

For the Filling:
2 cups heavy whipping cream
1 cup shredded white cheddar cheese
1 cup shredded Monterey Jack cheese
1/2 cup grated Parmesan cheese
1/2 cup crumbled goat cheese
1 cup crumbled Blue cheese
Salt & white pepper

Cook the pasta shells in salted boiling water until al dente. Drain well.

Preheat the oven to 375°F. Butter a 13x9-inch baking dish. Combine the panko crumbs and 1/2 cup Parmesan cheese and set aside.

continued

In a large pot over, medium heat, bring the cream to a simmer. Reduce the heat and add the white cheddar cheese, Jack cheese, remaining 1/2 cup of Parmesan cheese and the goat cheese. Stir slowly until all the cheeses melt. Add the blue cheese and cooked pasta and stir until combined. Season to taste with salt and pepper.

Pour the macaroni and cheese into the prepared pan and spread the bread crumb and Parmesan mixture evenly over the top. Bake uncovered, until golden and bubbly, about 20 minutes.

OUR TWO FAVORITE RISOTTOS

Winter is a great season to try as many Risotto recipes as possible.
Here are our two favorites!

MUSHROOM and ASPARAGUS RISOTTO Serves 6 as a Main Course or 4 as an Appetizer

Use an assortment of fresh and dried mushrooms when making this creamy Italian rice dish and be sure to use the soaking liquid from the reconstituted mushrooms in the risotto. Try morels, chanterelles, lobster or Portobello mushrooms for fabulous flavor.

6 cups chicken broth or vegetable broth
1/2 cup boiling water
2 ounces dried porcini mushrooms
1/4 cup extra-virgin olive oil
1 yellow onion, diced
1/2 pound white mushrooms, sliced
5 fresh shitake mushrooms, sliced
1/2 cup dry white wine
2 cups Arborio rice

1 bunch fresh asparagus,
**   stalks trimmed and cut into 1-inch pieces**
1/2 cup grated Parmesan cheese
Zest of 1 lemon
Salt & freshly ground pepper to taste

For Garnish:
3 tablespoons chopped fresh parsley

To reconstitute the dried mushrooms, pour the boiling water over the mushrooms and let soak for 15 minutes, then drain and reserve the soaking liquid.

Bring the broth to a simmer in a large saucepot. Heat the oil in a large high-sided sauté pan over medium heat. Add the onion and sauté until tender, about 10 minutes. Increase the heat to high, add the fresh mushrooms and sauté for 2 minutes. Add the dried mushrooms and season the mixture with salt and pepper. Add the rice and sauté 2 minutes more. Add the white wine and scrape up any caramelized bits from the bottom of the pan. Simmer the wine for 1 minute.

Add 2 large ladles full of stock at a time to the rice mixture. Over medium heat, stir the risotto constantly, adding the next ladle-full of stock only after the previous stock has been fully absorbed. Continue to add stock until the rice is creamy and cooked through, about 25 minutes total. Add the asparagus pieces during the last 10 minutes of cooking.

When ready to serve, stir in the cheese and lemon zest. Spoon into warm bowls and garnish with parsley.

SWEET CORN RISOTTO Serves 6 as a Main Course or 4 as an Appetizer

Lana's signature (and favorite "company") dish. She creates a spectacular entrée by garnishing each bowl with 1/4 cooked Maine Lobster per person, cooked, shelled and heated through in a little butter.

6 cups chicken broth or vegetable broth

5 ears fresh sweet corn, husked

4 tablespoons olive oil

2 shallots, minced

1/2 cup dry white wine

2 cups Arborio Rice

2 tablespoons mascarpone cheese

1/2 cup grated Parmesan cheese

1 teaspoon fresh tarragon, chopped

Salt & pepper

Bring the broth to a simmer in a large saucepot.

Cut the kernels from the ears of corn. Place the corn cobs into the simmering broth to infuse corn flavor into the liquid.

Heat the oil in a large high-sided sauté pan over medium heat. Add the shallots and sauté until tender, about 3 minutes. Add the rice and sauté 2 minutes more. Add the white wine and scrape up any caramelized bits from the bottom of the pan. Simmer the wine for 1 minute.

Add 2 large ladles full of stock at a time to the rice mixture. Over medium-low heat, stir the mixture constantly, adding the next ladle-full of stock only after the previous stock has been fully absorbed. Continue to add stock until the rice is creamy and cooked through, about 25 minutes total. Add the corn kernels during the last 5 minutes of cooking.

When ready to serve, stir in the mascarpone cheese, Parmesan cheese and tarragon. Spoon into warm bowls and serve.

LITTLE EARS with TOMATOES and TWO CHEESES Serves 4 to 6

Orecchiette (in Italian meaning "little ears") is a rustic Puglian-style pasta that perfectly captures cheesy and chunky sauces, due to its shape. Use any small pasta that holds sauce well if you can't find orecchiette.

2 cups cherry tomatoes, cut in half

2 garlic cloves, minced

12 fresh basil leaves, cut into thin strips

1/4 cup extra-virgin olive oil

1 pound orecchiette pasta

1/2 cup ricotta cheese

1/3 cup grated Parmesan cheese

Combine the tomato halves, garlic, basil and olive oil in a large mixing bowl and season with salt and pepper. Marinate at least 30 minutes at room temperature or overnight in the refrigerator. (Bring to room temperature before using.)

Cook the pasta in salted boiling water to the desired doneness. Drain the pasta and immediately add it to the room temperature tomato mixture. Stir in the ricotta and Parmesan cheeses.

Adjust the seasoning and serve immediately.

15-MINUTE LASAGNA Serves 6

It doesn't get any simpler than this! Frozen raviolis and prepared sauce make this a hassle-free version of everyone's favorite Italian recipe.

1/2 cup shredded Fontina cheese

1/2 cup shredded Mozzarella cheese

2 cups prepared pasta sauce

1 (30 ounce) bag frozen large cheese ravioli, kept frozen

1 (10 ounce) box frozen chopped spinach, thawed and squeezed dry

Grated Parmesan Cheese

Preheat the oven to 350°F. Combine the Fontina and Mozzarella cheese in a mixing bowl. Spread a thin layer of tomato sauce in a 13x9-inch baking dish. Top with a single layer of frozen raviolis, then top with a layer of cheese. Repeat, using the remaining ingredients, ending with cheese.

Cover the pan with foil and bake for 30 minutes. Uncover and bake 10 minutes more or until the cheese is melted and bubbly.

CHEF'S TIP:
Add crumbled cooked sausage, sautéed mushrooms, frozen chopped spinach (thawed)...just about anything, to embellish this luscious lasagna!

GIVING THANKS

CURRIED PUMPKIN SOUP

DUCK BREAST WITH CHERRY PORT SAUCE

CRANBERRY-ORANGE ROAST TURKEY

DRIED CHERRY, SAUSAGE AND CORNBREAD STUFFING

TWICE-BAKED MAPLE PECAN SWEET POTATOES

SPICED CRANBERRY SAUCE

PUMPKIN TIRAMISU

BROWN BUTTER PECAN PIE

DAY-AFTER TURKEY, APPLE & POTATO HASH

CURRIED PUMPKIN SOUP Serves 6

This soup can be made simple by using canned pumpkin puree. If you choose to make the bisque from scratch, use Sugar Pie Pumpkins, the small, sweet pumpkins that are available during holiday-time. Garnish each bowl with a sprinkling of roasted pumpkin seeds and a small dollop of crème fraiche. This luscious soup will keep in the fridge and it freezes well too.

1 (3 pound) pumpkin,
   halved lengthwise and cleaned
   or 2 cups canned pumpkin puree

1 tablespoon extra-virgin olive oil

2 tablespoons unsalted butter

1 yellow onion, diced

2 small pears, peeled,
   cored and cut into 1-inch chunks

3 garlic cloves, minced

1 tablespoon curry powder

1/2 cup dry white wine or apple juice

6 cups chicken broth

1/3 cup heavy whipping cream

Salt & freshly ground pepper

Garnish: Toasted pumpkin seeds
          Crème Fraiche or sour cream

If using a whole pumpkin, place the pumpkin halves, cut side down, on a baking sheet and pour a half cup of water onto the baking sheet. Cover the pan with foil and bake at 350°F for about 1 hour, or until the pumpkin flesh is tender when pierced with a knife. When cool enough to handle, scrape the pumpkin flesh from the skins.

Heat the oil and butter in a large stockpot. Add the onion and sauté over medium heat until tender, about 8 minutes. Add the pears, garlic and curry powder to the pot and cook 2 minutes more. Season with salt & pepper. Add the wine or juice and deglaze, scraping up any caramelized bits on the bottom of the pot. Add the roasted pumpkin and the chicken broth and bring the soup to a boil. Reduce the heat to medium-low and simmer for 45 minutes.

Puree the soup in batches in a blender until smooth, or use an immersion blender to puree the soup in the pot. Return the pureed soup to the pot and heat thoroughly. Stir in the cream and adjust the seasoning. Do not boil.

Serve the soup in warm bowls garnished with a dollop of cream and a few pumpkin seeds.

DUCK BREAST with CHERRY PORT SAUCE   Serves 4

Simply scrumptious, duck is remarkably lean and much more flavorful than chicken. While Muscovy duck has the best flavor, any breed of duck is fine in this dish and frozen duck breasts are perfectly adequate. Make sure that they are completely thawed before marinating them.

1 cup Cabernet Sauvignon	1 cup Port
2 garlic cloves, minced	1 cup chicken broth
1 shallot, minced	3/4 cup dried cherries
4 fresh sage leaves, chopped	2 tablespoons brown sugar
2 sprigs of thyme, picked and chopped	3 fresh sage leaves, left whole
4 duck breasts (6 to 8 ounces each)	3 tablespoons unsalted butter,
Salt & freshly ground pepper	cubed and kept cold

Combine the wine, garlic, shallot, sage and thyme. Cut horizontal slits in the skin of each duck breast (do not pierce the meat) and place the duck breasts in a shallow pan. Cover with the wine mixture and marinate overnight in the fridge.

Drain the duck breasts from the marinade and season the duck with salt and pepper. In a dry sauté pan over medium heat, place the duck breasts skin side down. Cook the Muscovy duck breast for about 10 minutes, the individual breasts for 3 minutes, or until the skin is crisp and mahogany-colored. Turn the breasts over and cook 4 minutes longer for the small breasts or 10 minutes longer for the Muscovy breast, for medium rare, or to the desired doneness. Remove the duck from the pan and keep warm and carefully pour off the fat from the pan.

Increase the heat to high and add the Port to the same sauté pan. Simmer until reduced by one-half. Add the chicken broth, cherries, brown sugar and sage leaves and simmer the mixture until reduced by half. Remove the pan from the heat, discard the sage leaves and whisk in the cold butter. Season the sauce with salt and pepper.

Slice the duck breasts on the bias and serve with the sauce.

CRANBERRY-ORANGE ROAST TURKEY Serves 10 to 12

Not your ordinary holiday turkey, this recipe is robust with flavor. The method requires roasting the turkey covered, therefore steaming it, to create a succulent, moist, juicy bird. The steaming process makes it easy on the cook too, as the turkey should roast for 2 1/2 full hours without opening the oven. Be sure to prepare your stuffing in a separate pan, as this turkey is not meant to be stuffed.

1 (14 to 16 pound) Turkey

Salt & freshly ground pepper

2 tablespoons garlic powder

3 yellow onions, diced

2 (15 ounce) cans whole berry
   cranberry sauce

1 cup orange marmalade

1 cup teriyaki sauce

1 cup honey

Juice of two oranges

1 cup water

1 handful mixed fresh herbs – sage, rosemary, parsley

Preheat the oven to 425°F. Clean the turkey well and dry completely. Season the entire bird with salt, pepper and the garlic powder. Spray a large roasting pan (preferably one with a lid, or you can use heavy duty aluminum foil) and the inside of the lid with non-stick cooking spray. Place the diced onions on the bottom of the roasting pan. Set the seasoned turkey on top of the onions.

In a large mixing bowl, whisk together the cranberry sauce, marmalade, teriyaki sauce, honey, orange juice and water until well blended. Stuff the juiced orange rinds inside the cavity of the turkey for moisture. Pour the mixture over the turkey. Place the fresh herbs on top of the turkey. Tightly secure the lid or cover the roasting pan with heavy-duty aluminum foil. Be sure to cover the pan tightly to keep any steam from escaping.

Roast the turkey for 2 1/2 hours. Do not open the lid during cooking. After 2 1/2 hours of cooking, reduce the oven temperature to 350°F and remove the lid or foil from the pan. Remove the herbs from the top of the turkey and discard. Continue roasting the turkey, uncovered, for about 30 minutes more, or until the turkey is golden brown and cooked through completely. (To test the doneness: a meat thermometer inserted into the thickest part of the thigh, without touching the bone, should register 180°F.)

Allow the turkey to rest for 20 minutes before carving.

WINE TIP:

To compliment your Thanksgiving feast, a fine bubbly makes a wonderful companion. You could choose to serve Champagne or Sparkling Wine all throughout the meal for a perfect pairing. As for white wine, an oaky Chardonnay (often the faithful standby), is not ideal for a holiday feast. Consider a fruity or tangy white such as a Viognier, Sauvignon Blanc or a Riesling. For red, a Cab might be too big and bold to match a multitude of dishes. Try pairing a Pinot Noir, Syrah or a Beaujolais Nouveau (often called the "perfect" Thanksgiving wine). Serve the Beaujolais slightly chilled.

DRIED CHERRY, SAUSAGE and CORNBREAD STUFFING   Serves 10

Did you know that if the mixture is baked inside the turkey, it's called stuffing, but if it's not, it's called dressing? Dried cranberries or dried apricots add terrific flavor, as well as diced apples or pears. Use store bought or homemade cornbread.

2 pounds prepared cornbread, cubed	2 medium onions, diced
1 cup dried cherries	6 celery stalks, diced
1/2 cup Grand Marnier	1/4 cup chopped fresh parsley
1 stick (4 ounces) unsalted butter	Salt & freshly ground pepper
1/2 pound mild Italian sausage, casings removed	2 cups chicken broth

Preheat the oven to 350°F. Place the cornbread cubes in a single layer on baking sheets and toast the cornbread cubes in the oven until crisp, about 20 minutes, tossing a few times during cooking. Transfer the cubes to a large mixing bowl. Maintain the oven temperature.

Place the cherries and Grand Marnier in a small saucepot. Bring to a boil, then remove from the heat. Allow the cherries to plump for 15 minutes.

In a large sauté pan, cook the sausage, crumbling the sausage as it cooks, until golden brown and cooked through. Using a slotted spoon, remove the crumbled sausage and add it to the toasted cornbread.

In the same saucepan, melt the butter over medium heat. Add the onions and celery and sauté until tender, stirring often, about 15 minutes. Season with salt and pepper to taste.

Add the sautéed mixture to the cornbread and crumbled sausage along with the parsley. Add the plumped cherries, along with the soaking liquid. Add enough chicken broth to moisten the stuffing. Mix to combine well.

If you are stuffing and roasting your turkey, be sure to cool the stuffing mixture to room temperature before stuffing your turkey.

Generously butter a 13x9-inch baking dish. Transfer the stuffing to the prepared dish. Cover with foil, and bake until heated through, about 45 minutes. Uncover and bake until the top is crisp and golden, about 15 minutes longer.

TWICE-BAKED MAPLE PECAN
SWEET POTATOES Serves 8

The sweet potato filling in this recipe can be made up to 2 days ahead. Refrigerate the filling in an airtight container and bring the mixture to room temperature before stuffing the potato skins and baking.

8 large sweet potatoes

1/2 cup evaporated milk

1 stick (4 ounces) unsalted butter, melted

1/4 cup maple syrup

3 tablespoons firmly packed brown sugar

1 teaspoon pure vanilla extract

1/2 teaspoon ground cinnamon

Salt & freshly ground pepper

1 1/2 cups coarsely chopped pecans

Preheat the oven to 350°F.

Prick the sweet potatoes with a fork, to allow the steam to escape. Wrap each sweet potato in aluminum foil and place the wrapped potatoes on a baking sheet. Roast the sweet potatoes for 1 hour or until tender. Maintain the oven temperature.

Let the potatoes cool slightly, then cut a thin lengthwise slice from the top of each sweet potato. Scoop out the flesh, leaving a thin shell. Place the shells on a baking sheet lined with a silicone baking mat or parchment paper and set aside.

In a large mixing bowl, whisk together the evaporated milk, butter, maple syrup, brown sugar, vanilla and cinnamon. Add the cooked sweet potato flesh and salt and pepper and mix well to combine.

Spoon the mixture into the potato shells. Top each with a sprinkling of pecans and bake for 30 minutes, or until bubbly.

SPICED CRANBERRY SAUCE Serves 6 to 8

This simple homemade cranberry sauce is so flavorful and fresh tasting you will never go back to canned again!

> 2 cups fresh orange juice
>
> 2 (12 ounce) bags fresh cranberries
>
> 1 cup golden raisins
>
> 2 teaspoons pumpkin pie spice
>
> 2 cups granulated sugar
>
> Zest of 2 oranges
>
> 1 cup chopped walnuts, toasted (optional)
>
> Pinch of salt

Combine the orange juice, cranberries, raisins and pumpkin pie spice in a saucepot. Bring to a boil, then reduce the heat to simmer and cook for 10 minutes. Remove from heat. Add the sugar, orange zest, walnuts and salt and mix well. Allow the mixture to cool, then refrigerate overnight before serving.

CHEF'S TIP:

The trick to tender cranberries is to add the sugar after the cranberries have softened, which keep the skins from getting tough.

PUMPKIN TIRAMISU Serves 8

This simple and delicious twist on the classic is layered in individual martini glasses or a trifle bowl. We mix mascarpone cheese with pumpkin puree to create raves from your guests.

> 1 standard-sized loaf Pound Cake or 3 packages ladyfingers
>
> 2 cups heavy whipping cream
>
> 1 cup (8 ounces) mascarpone cheese
>
> 1/2 cup pumpkin puree
>
> 2/3 cup powdered sugar
>
> 1/2 teaspoon freshly grated nutmeg
>
> 1/2 teaspoon ground cinnamon
>
> 1/2 teaspoon pure vanilla extract
>
> 1/4 cup Frangelico Liqueur, Butterscotch Schnapps, Grand
>   Marnier or orange juice

If using Pound cake, slice the cake into 1/2-inch thick slices, then cut each slice vertically into three strips.

Using an electric mixer, or by hand, whip the cream to stiff peaks.

In a mixing bowl, combine the mascarpone, pumpkin puree, sugar, nutmeg, cinnamon and vanilla and blend well. Gently stir in 1 cup of the whipped cream.

To assemble the Tiramisu, place 8 martini or large-mouthed wine glasses on a work surface. In assembly line fashion, place a few pound cake pieces or ladyfingers in the bottom of each glass. Brush the cake with the liqueur of your choice, then top with a layer of the pumpkin cream mixture. Repeat layering, ending with the pumpkin mixture. Top each glass with a dollop of whipped cream. Chill before serving.

CHEF'S TIP:
Double the recipe to fill a large trifle bowl and garnish the top of the trifle with crushed gingersnaps or strips of candied ginger.

BROWN BUTTER PECAN PIE Serves 8

At Thanksgiving, I serve this pie warm with vanilla bean ice cream and a big bowl of maple-flavored whipped cream. Browning the butter creates a wonderfully nutty flavor and along with the addition of maple syrup, makes the pie truly irresistible.

For the Crust:
1 1/3 cups all-purpose flour
1/4 cup granulated sugar
1 stick (4 ounces) unsalted butter, cold and cut into small pieces
1 large egg yolk

For the Filling:
1 3/4 cups pecan halves
6 tablespoons unsalted butter
3 large eggs
2 tablespoons all-purpose flour
1 cup firmly packed brown sugar
1/3 cup pure maple syrup
1 teaspoon pure vanilla extract
Pinch of salt

To make the crust, preheat the oven to 300°F. Combine the flour and sugar in the bowl of a food processor. Pulse to combine. Add the cold butter and pulse until fine crumbs form. Add the egg yolk and pulse just until the dough holds together. Press the dough into the bottom and up the sides of a 9-inch pie pan or a springform pan. Bake the crust for 25 minutes or until light golden. (You can make the crust ahead of time, bake it and either store it at room temperature for 1 day or freeze it until ready to use. Be sure to thaw the frozen baked crust, unwrapped completely, before baking.)

To make the filling, preheat the oven to 350°F. Spread the pecans on a baking sheet in a single layer and bake until fragrant and toasted, about 10 minutes. Using a food processor, finely grind 1/4 cup of the toasted pecans.

In a small sauté pan cook the butter over medium-low heat until it begins to brown and have a nutty aroma. Remove from the heat and set aside.

In a large mixing bowl, whisk the eggs to blend. Add the ground pecans, toasted pecan halves, browned butter, flour, brown sugar, maple syrup, vanilla and salt. Mix well.

Pour the filling into the prepared crust. Bake the pie until the center is set, about 30 minutes. Remove the pie from the oven and allow it to cool at least 30 minutes before slicing.

DAY AFTER TURKEY, APPLE & POTATO HASH Serves 4

This delicious breakfast or brunch dish is the perfect way to use up leftover turkey. Simple and easy to make, this is a wonderful start to any fall day. For my signature hash I add caramelized onions and a few strips of crumbled bacon.

1 bag (20 ounce) frozen hash brown potatoes, thawed

4 cups cooked leftover turkey, diced

1 green apple – cored, seeded and diced

3 tablespoons chopped fresh parsley

1/3 cup chicken broth

3 tablespoons heavy whipping cream

1/2 teaspoon ground sage

Salt & freshly ground pepper

1/4 cup vegetable oil

Combine the thawed hash browns, turkey, apple, parsley, chicken broth, cream and sage and salt and pepper in a large mixing bowl. Gently toss to combine.

Heat a large sauté pan over medium heat. Add the oil and heat until almost smoking. Add the potato mixture and spread evenly in the pan. Cover the pan and cook for 15 minutes, stirring occasionally. Remove the lid, increase the heat to high and cook the hash for an additional 10 minutes or until crisp and golden brown.

Spreading Good Cheer

CHOCOLATE-DIPPED PEPPERMINT PRETZELS

~~~~~~~

CASHEW BRITTLE

~~~~~~~

ORANGE SHORTBREAD COOKIES

~~~~~~~

ITALIAN ALMOND COOKIES

~~~~~~~

SWEET AND SPICY MIXED NUTS

CHOCOLATE-DIPPED PEPPERMINT PRETZELS Makes 24 Pretzels

A delightful treat for the kid in all of us! The combination of the salty pretzels with the sweet chocolate and the spicy candy is delectable. Pack these festive goodies in candy bags and give them as gifts or set them out on the dessert buffet at your holiday party.

1 cup peppermint candies or candy canes, crushed

12 ounces bittersweet or semi-sweet chocolate, chopped

24 large Bavarian Pretzels

Place the crushed peppermint candies on a large plate.

In a double boiler, melt the chocolate until smooth. Or, melt the chocolate in the microwave on 50% power, in 30-second increments, until melted.

Dunk each pretzel three-quarters of the way into the melted chocolate. Immediately roll the chocolate-coated pretzel in the candy bits. Transfer the pretzels to a silicone-lined or parchment paper-lined baking sheet to allow the chocolate to set. Store airtight at room temperature.

CASHEW BRITTLE Serves 6 to 8

This "Made in the Microwave" recipe makes a great treat for Halloween, Christmas or any occasion. We also use the large broken pieces of brittle to decorate cupcakes or large frosted cakes.

1 cup whole cashew nuts

1 cup granulated sugar

1/2 cup light corn syrup

1/8 teaspoon salt

1 teaspoon unsalted butter

1 teaspoon pure vanilla extract

1 teaspoon baking soda

Combine the cashews, sugar, corn syrup and salt in a 1 1/2-quart microwave-safe bowl. Microwave on High (100% power) for 4 minutes, remove and stir well, then return to the microwave and for cook 3 minutes more.

Carefully remove the hot bowl from the microwave and stir in the butter and vanilla. Microwave for 1 minute more; cashews should be lightly browned and the syrup should be golden in color. Carefully remove the hot bowl and add the baking soda. Gently stir until light and foamy.

Immediately pour the mixture onto a lightly greased or silicone mat-lined baking sheet and let cool for 30 minutes. When the brittle has hardened, break it into shards and store in an airtight container at room temperature.

CHEF'S TIP:
Use raw peanuts, hazelnuts, almonds or macadamia nuts, in place of the cashews, if desired. If you're using roasted nuts, reduce the initial cooking time by one minute.

ORANGE SHORTBREAD COOKIES Makes about 3 dozen cookies

These flaky, buttery cookies are enhanced by fresh orange zest and topped off with a coating of luscious chocolate.

2 sticks (8 ounces) unsalted butter, at room temperature

1/2 cup powdered sugar

1/2 teaspoon pure vanilla extract

1/4 teaspoon almond extract

Juice and zest of 1 orange

2 1/2 cups all-purpose flour

1 teaspoon salt

12 ounces high-quality bittersweet chocolate, chopped

   (I prefer Valrhona, Scharffenberger or Callebaut)

Using an electric mixer, beat the butter until light and fluffy. Gradually beat in the powdered sugar. Add the vanilla and almond extract, orange juice and orange zest and blend well. Add the flour and salt and stir just until combined. Gather the dough into a ball and split it into two even pieces. Flatten each piece into a disk and wrap individually in plastic wrap. Refrigerate the dough until firm, about 1 hour.

When ready to bake, preheat the oven to 325°F. Line 3 baking sheets with silicone baking mats or parchment paper. On a lightly floured surface, roll out one disk of the dough to 1/4-inch thickness. Cut out the cookies using a round cutter and place the cut-outs on the prepared cookie sheet. Gather the scraps from the dough, re-roll and continue to cut out cookies. Repeat with the remaining disk of dough. Bake the cookies for 20 to 25 minutes or until the edges begin to brown. Remove the cookies from the oven and allow them to cool to room temperature.

When the cookies are completely cool, melt the chocolate in a shallow bowl. Dip each cookie in the melted chocolate to cover half of the cookie. Place the dipped cookies on a silicone-lined or parchment paper-lined baking sheet to allow the chocolate to set. Store the cookies in an airtight container.

ITALIAN ALMOND COOKIES Makes about 24 Cookies

These delicious Amaretti cookies are a lovely gift put into small candy bags and tied with a ribbon. They taste especially delicious served with coffee, tea or after dinner drinks and they make a wonderful topping to a trifle or custard. For a savory use, crumble the cookies over cheese or pumpkin ravioli.

7 ounces raw almonds

1 cup superfine sugar

1/4 cup all-purpose flour

2 egg whites

1/2 teaspoon almond extract

Pinch of salt

Coarse sugar crystals, for the tops of the cookies

Preheat the oven to 350°F.

Place the almonds and sugar in the bowl of a food processor and process until the almonds are roughly chopped. Add the flour, egg whites, almond extract and salt and process until well combined.

Roll the dough into tablespoon size balls and place on a baking sheet lined with a silicone baking mat or parchment paper. Using wet fingertips, flatten the balls slightly then top each cookie with a sprinkling of coarse sugar.

Bake the cookies for 15 to 20 minutes or until light golden in color. Cool completely on the baking sheet before removing.

SWEET AND SPICY MIXED NUTS

Makes 4 Cups

Serve this addictive sweet, spicy and salty snack with cocktails or give them as gifts in a holiday tin (they make a great garnish for salads too!). Whenever we serve these heavenly nuts at parties, we have so many guests ask for the recipe that we now have printouts ready!

1 large egg white

1 teaspoon water

4 cups mixed salted roasted nuts

1 cup granulated sugar

3 teaspoons 5-Spice powder, pumpkin pie spice or chipotle powder

Preheat the oven to 350°F.

Whisk together the egg white and water in a large bowl until frothy. Stir in nuts and toss to coat. In a separate bowl combine the sugar and your spice of choice. Stir the spice mixture into the nuts, coating well.

Spread the nuts in a single layer onto a baking sheet and bake for 15 to 20 minutes, stirring once, or until fragrant and golden.

CHEF'S TIP:

The nuts will keep for a few weeks in an airtight container at room temperature before losing flavor. I like to use a combination of cashews, almonds, hazelnuts and pistachios.

SPECIAL CELEBRATION SWEETS

BLUM'S COFFEE CRUNCH CAKE

~~~~~

CHOCOLATE BREAD PUDDING WITH SEA SALT CARAMEL SAUCE

~~~~~

GINGERBREAD STARS

~~~~~

PEANUT BUTTER CHOCOLATE CHEESECAKE

~~~~~

TOFFEE BROWNIES

~~~~~

CHOCOLATE RASPBERRY CLAFOUTIS

~~~~~

TRIPLE CHOCOLATE OVERLOAD ICE CREAM PIE

BLUM'S COFFEE CRUNCH CAKE Makes One 10-inch Cake

This is one delicious cake, full of fond memories (and its one of Lana's favorite desserts!). It hails from the popular but long-shuttered Blum's pastry shops in San Francisco. If you are time challenged, many people use a store-bought angel food cake and make the rest.

For the Cake:
2 1/4 cups cake flour
1 1/2 cups granulated sugar
1 tablespoon baking powder
1 teaspoon salt
3/4 cup water
1/2 cup vegetable oil
6 large eggs, separated
Zest of 1 lemon
1 tablespoon pure vanilla extract

For the Coffee Frosting:
1 1/2 cups heavy whipping cream
1/4 cup strong brewed coffee
3 tablespoons superfine sugar

For the Coffee Crunch:
Vegetable oil, for baking sheet
1 1/2 cups granulated sugar
1/4 cup strong brewed coffee
1/4 cup light corn syrup
1 tablespoon baking soda

Preheat the oven to 325°F. Sift together the flour, 3/4 cup sugar, baking powder and salt in a large mixing bowl. Add the water, oil, egg yolks, zest and vanilla and beat until smooth.

In the bowl of an electric mixer beat the egg whites on medium-high speed until frothy. With the mixer running, add the remaining 3/4 cup sugar in a slow steady stream and beat until stiff glossy peaks form.

Fold the beaten egg whites into the batter in two additions. Pour the batter into a nonstick 10-inch tube pan. Bake until a cake tester inserted in the center comes out clean, about 1 hour. Remove the cake from the oven, and invert onto a narrow-necked bottle. Let stand until cool, about 1 hour, before removing the pan.

To make the Coffee Frosting, in the bowl of an electric mixer whip the cream until stiff peaks form. Add the coffee and sugar, and beat to combine. Use immediately.

Place the cake on a serving platter. Cover the cake with an even layer of frosting. Just before serving, sprinkle the top and sides of the cake generously with Coffee Crunch.

To make the Coffee Crunch, lightly coat a rimmed baking sheet with oil.

In a 4-quart saucepan, combine the sugar, coffee, and corn syrup. Bring the mixture to a boil and cook over medium heat until the mixture registers 310°F on a candy thermometer.

Remove the pan from the heat and sprinkle the baking soda evenly over the sugar syrup. Stir just until combined. Pour the mixture immediately onto the prepared baking sheet. Let stand until cool, about 30 minutes.

When ready to use, tap the Coffee Crunch lightly with a spoon or knife handle to crack. Break the Crunch into irregular 1/4-to-1/2-inch pieces.

CHOCOLATE BREAD PUDDING
with SEA SALT CARAMEL SAUCE Serves 8

Simple to prepare and a definite crowd pleaser....Absolutely wonderful!

6 cups Sweet Hawaiian Bread or Brioche, cut into 1-inch cubes
3/4 cup granulated sugar
1 cup heavy whipping cream
3 whole eggs
1 teaspoon pure vanilla extract
1/2 teaspoon ground cinnamon
Pinch of salt
8 ounces bittersweet chocolate, broken into pieces

Place the bread cubes into an 8x8-inch baking dish; do not pack them in. Sporadically place the chocolate pieces in between the crevices of the top layer of bread.

In a mixing bowl, whisk together the sugar, cream, eggs, vanilla, cinnamon and salt. Pour the mixture over the bread and let stand for 15 minutes to allow the bread to soak up the custard. Preheat the oven to 375°F.

Bake for 35 to 40 minutes or until the bread pudding is golden and the custard is set. Remove from the oven and serve with the Praline sauce.

SEA SALT CARAMEL SAUCE

This sweet and slightly salty sauce is the perfect compliment to the bread pudding and it makes a luscious topping for Banana Tartlets and Ice Cream Sundaes.

1 stick (4 ounces) unsalted butter
1/2 cup brown sugar
1/2 cup heavy whipping cream
A liberal pinch of sea salt

Combine all of the ingredients in a saucepan and bring to a boil over high heat. Reduce the heat to low and simmer for 5 minutes. Serve hot.

GINGERBREAD STARS Serves 8 (with scraps for midnight snacking!)

This rich, moist and spicy gingerbread is best made a day ahead and it keeps well at room temperature for up to a week without losing flavor. Serve it for dessert, cut into star shapes, for a Tea, cut into small squares and be sure to use any leftover gingerbread in a Trifle, layered with whipped cream and candied fruit.

2 cups all-purpose flour	1 stick (4 ounces) unsalted butter
2 teaspoons ground ginger	1 cup dark brown sugar
1 1/2 teaspoons baking soda	3 large eggs
1 teaspoon cinnamon	1 cup molasses
1/2 teaspoon ground cloves	1 cup dark beer
1/2 teaspoon nutmeg	Confectioners' sugar, for dusting
Pinch of salt	Whipped cream, for serving

Preheat the oven to 350°F. Generously grease a 13x9-inch baking pan.

In a medium bowl, sift together the flour, ginger, baking soda, cinnamon, cloves, nutmeg and salt.

Using an electric mixer cream together the butter and brown sugar until fluffy. Add the eggs one at a time, beating well after each addition. Add the molasses and blend well.

Add the dry ingredients and the beer alternately to the butter mixture, beating well after each addition.

Pour the batter into the prepared pan and bake for 40 minutes or until a cake tester comes out with just a few crumbs sticking to it. Remove the cake from the oven and allow it to cool completely in the pan.

Using a star-shaped cookie cutter, cut out individual portions of the gingerbread. Dust each star with confectioners' sugar and serve with a dollop of whipped cream.

PEANUT BUTTER CHOCOLATE CHEESECAKE Serves 8 to 10

Use a knife dipped in hot water to slice this luscious cheesecake and decorate each slice with whipped cream and chocolate curls. It's best made a day or two ahead.

For the Crust:

1 1/2 cups unsalted peanuts

1/4 cup granulated sugar

1 1/2 tablespoons unsweetened
  cocoa powder

4 tablespoons unsalted butter, melted

For the Filling:

24 ounces cream cheese, at room temperature

1 1/2 cups firmly packed brown sugar

1/2 cup creamy peanut butter

1 teaspoon pure vanilla extract

4 large eggs

1/4 cup heavy whipping cream

1/2 cup chocolate chips

1/2 cup peanut butter chips

Preheat the oven to 350°F.

For the Crust, combine the peanuts, sugar and cocoa in a food processor. Pulse until the peanuts are finely ground. Add the melted butter and pulse to combine. Press the mixture onto the bottom and one inch up the sides of a 10-inch spring-form pan.

To make the filling, using an electric mixer beat the cream cheese and brown sugar until smooth. Add the peanut butter and vanilla and beat just until blended. Add the eggs 1 at a time, beating after each addition. Add the cream and beat until smooth. By hand, stir in the chocolate chips and peanut butter chips.

Pour the filling into the crust and bake for 1 hour or until just set (the center might still be slightly loose). Cool the cheesecake in the pan on a rack then cover and refrigerate overnight.

CHEF'S TIP:

A Bain Marie, the French term for "Water Bath", is a cooking method used for cheesecakes and delicate custards to lessen cracking and make for more even cooking. Wrap the bottom of the springform pan with aluminum foil to keep the water from seeping into the pan. Place the springform pan, once filled with batter, inside a large roasting pan and place it in the oven. Pull the oven rack out so that the roasting pan is halfway out of the oven and from a tea kettle or measuring cup, pour boiling water into the roasting pan to surround the cheesecake. Fill the water to 2-inches up the sides of the springform pan. Carefully push the rack back into the oven and bake accordingly.

TOFFEE BROWNIES Serves 6 to 8

Moist, fudgy and chewy, these brownies are packed with lots of toffee chunks. We recommend that you do not use prepackaged toffee bits, as they don't have enough chocolate coating! Buy Heath Bars (which are chocolate covered) and chop them into chunks. Store the brownies airtight, at room temperature, for up to 2 days or they freeze perfectly for longer storage. We like to bake these brownies a day ahead for better flavor and texture.

8 (1.4 ounce) chocolate-covered toffee bars

5 ounces unsweetened chocolate, chopped

1 1/2 sticks (12 ounces) unsalted butter, cut into

1 1/2 cups granulated sugar

1 teaspoon pure vanilla extract

3 large eggs, at room temperature

3/4 cup plus 3 tablespoons all-purpose flour

Pinch of salt

Line a brownie pan, at least 1-1/2 inches deep, with heavy-duty aluminum foil. Preheat the oven to 350°F.

By hand, chop the toffee bars into chunks.

In a double boiler, melt the chocolate until smooth. Or, melt the chocolate in the microwave on 50% power, in 30-second increments, until melted. Add the sugar and vanilla and stir in until well combined. Beat in the eggs, one at a time, then add the flour and salt and stir just until blended. Fold in the toffee chunks by hand.

Spoon the batter into the prepared pan and spread the batter evenly into the corners of the pan. Bake for 20 minutes, turning the pan around halfway during baking. A cake tester inserted 1-inch from the edge of the pan should come out with only a few crumbs. Do not overbake!

Cool the brownies completely at room temperature before cutting. Remove the block of brownies in the foil and peel back the foil from the sides. Cut the brownies using a sharp straight-edged knife.

CHOCOLATE RASPBERRY CLAFOUTIS Serves 8

A Clafoutis is a baked custard-like French dessert that is made by pouring a loose batter over fresh fruit (traditionally fresh cherries). You can substitute other fruit such as strawberries, blueberries, apricots, figs, fresh cherries or canned cherries or even sliced stone fruit. An easy recipe with impressive results!

2 pints fresh raspberries

4 large eggs

1 cup whole milk

1/2 teaspoon almond extract

3/4 cup all-purpose flour

2/3 cup granulated sugar

4 ounces bittersweet chocolate, chopped finely

For Garnish: Vanilla Ice Cream or Whipped Cream

Preheat the oven to 350°F.

Butter a 10-inch ceramic baking dish and place the raspberries in the dish. In a large mixing bowl, whisk together the eggs, milk, almond extract, flour and sugar until smooth. Pour the batter over the raspberries. Sprinkle the surface of the batter with the chocolate.

Bake the Clafoutis for 40 minutes. Cool slightly, cut into wedges and serve topped with ice cream or whipped cream.

TRIPLE CHOCOLATE OVERLOAD
ICE CREAM PIE Serves 8

A chocolate cookie crust, three kinds of chocolate ice cream and chocolate sauce....Chocolate overkill at its finest! Plan to prepare this decadent dessert early in the day or the night before, as it does need time in the freezer to set completely.

For the Crust:

25 Oreo cookies

4 tablespoons unsalted butter, melted

For the Chocolate Sauce:

1 1/2 cups heavy whipping cream

4 tablespoons unsalted butter

4 tablespoons light corn syrup

1 pound (16 ounces) bittersweet or
   semi-sweet chocolate, chopped

2 teaspoons pure vanilla extract

For the Filling:

3 pints Chocolate Ice Cream
   (6 cups total)

*Pick 3 of your favorite Ice Cream
   flavors...Chocolate, Rocky Road,
   Chocolate Chip, Cookies & Cream,
   Marble Fudge

To make the crust, using a food processor, finely grind the Oreo cookies. Remove 2 tablespoons of the Oreo crumbs and set them aside for later use. Add the melted butter to the remaining crumbs and pulse to combine. Press the crumb mixture onto the bottom and up the sides of a 9-inch pie pan.

Freeze the crust until firm, about 15 minutes.

To make the Chocolate Sauce, combine the cream, butter and corn syrup in a medium saucepan. Bring the mixture to a boil, then remove from the heat. Add the chopped chocolate and vanilla and let stand 1 minute. Whisk until smooth. Let the sauce stand at room temperature for 20 minutes, or until slightly thickened.

To assemble the pie, spread 2 cups of your first ice cream flavor onto the chilled crust. Drizzle 1/2 cup of the chocolate sauce over the ice cream. Freeze the pie for 15 minutes or until the sauce sets. Spread your next ice cream flavor to create the next layer. Top with another 1/2 cup of chocolate sauce and freeze again for 15 minutes to set. Finally, top the pie with your last ice cream flavor, mounding it in the center to create a dome shape. Sprinkle the reserved Oreo cookie crumbs over the top of the pie. Freeze the pie until firm, about 2 hours. If not serving immediately, cover the pie with plastic wrap and return to the freezer.

To serve the pie, heat the remaining chocolate sauce over low heat until warm. Slice and serve the ice cream pie with the warm chocolate sauce.

A Toast To... Drink & Cocktails

CHAMPAGNE PUNCH

~~~~~

LANA'S LIMÓNCELLO

~~~~~

CANDIED GINGER VODKA

~~~~~

FROZEN WATERMELON MARGARITAS

~~~~~

JAVATINI

~~~~~

MINTED VANILLA LEMONADE

CHAMPAGNE PUNCH

A great party always needs a great punch...and this punch is also the perfect way to toast in the New Year. For a special kid's punch, try mixing ginger ale and pineapple juice, in equal parts, and float scoops of rainbow sherbet on top....just for fun!

> 1 cup Brandy
>
> 1 cup Triple Sec
>
> 2 cups crushed pineapple in heavy syrup, drained
>
> 4 cups chilled ginger ale
>
> 2 (750-ml.) bottles dry or Brut Champagne, chilled

In a pitcher combine the Brandy, Triple Sec and crushed pineapple and chill the mixture for at least 2 hours. In a large punch bowl combine the brandy mixture, ginger ale and Champagne. Serve immediately.

LANA'S LIMÓNCELLO Makes 2 Quarts

This Italian spirit is best served well chilled as an after dinner drink. Lemon flavored liqueur dates back many centuries and is based on an age old method of combining an infusion of sugar, water and lemon with a natural spirit. Make this for your own festivities or give it as a gift at the holidays.

> 2 pounds lemons
>
> 1 quart (32 ounces) good-quality Vodka
>
> 2 cups granulated sugar
>
> 4 cups water

Using a vegetable peeler or a very sharp pairing knife, remove only the yellow peel from the lemons. Combine the lemon peels and the vodka in a nonreactive sealable container and store in a cool, dry place for 3 days, making sure to shake the bottle once a day. Once the alcohol has been infused with the lemon peel (the color should transfer from the peels to the vodka), remove the peels from the vodka and discard.

In a saucepan over low heat, combine the sugar and water and heat the mixture over medium heat until the sugar dissolves and the syrup is clear. Let the mixture cool to room temperature then mix it with the infused alcohol. Store the Limóncello in the freezer.

CANDIED GINGER VODKA Makes 1 Liter

The sweet and spicy flavor of candied ginger adds an Asian-fusion elegance to any cocktail. For different vodka variations, try infusing your liter of vodka with two cups of fresh mint leaves or two vanilla beans, or add 25 coffee beans for a coffee flavored vodka. Steep for at least 1 week and up to 2 weeks, as needed.

> **1 pound (16 ounces) candied ginger**
> **1 liter good-quality Vodka**

Combine the candied ginger and Vodka in a covered container and store in a cool, dark place for 2 weeks.

Strain the Vodka and chill thoroughly before serving.

FROZEN WATERMELON MARGARITAS Makes 4 Margaritas….Multiply as necessary!

A refreshing pitcher of pureed Watermelon Margaritas tastes especially delicious on a hot day!

> **6 ounces Tequila**
> **3 ounces Triple sec**
> **1 cup Homemade Sweet & Sour Mix**
>   **(see the "It's A Housewarming Chapter")**
> **3 cups cubed & seeded watermelon**
> **4 cups ice cubes**

Combine all of the ingredients in a blender and blend until smooth. Serve in chilled glasses garnished with slices of watermelon.

JAVATINI Makes 2 Cocktails

This is the ultimate dessert Martini! There are two types of Martinis: The Gin Martini and the Vodka Martini....We recommend that you stick with a vodka base for this drink. Serve this decadent drink with my Bittersweet Chocolate Truffles or our Orange Shortbread Cookies.

4 ounces Vodka

2 ounces Kahlua

2 ounces brewed Espresso, cooled

Combine the vodka, Kahlua and espresso in a cocktail shaker with ice. Serve straight-up in cocoa-rimmed martini glasses. Garnish with chocolate shavings.

MINTED VANILLA LEMONADE (Non-Alcoholic & Sugar Free)

Pour into ice-filled glasses and garnish with a sprig of mint.

1 cup SPLENDA

1 cup water

2 cups freshly lemon juice

2 pints fresh strawberries, hulled and quartered

30 fresh mint leaves

1 vanilla bean, split and scraped

1 orange, sliced

1 lemon sliced

4 cups water

To make the Splenda Simple Syrup, combine the Splenda and water in a small saucepan and bring to a boil. Stir until the Splenda has completely dissolved.

Combine the prepared Splenda simple syrup with the remaining ingredients in a pitcher and allow the mixture to sit at room temperature for 4 hours or in the refrigerator overnight. Serve over ice.

INDEX